Grace Crawforth

bought at Bradford
when staying with Ethel
September 1943

COUNTRY MOODS AND TENSES

1   Village Cricket at Hughenden, Bucks, *ca.* 1857

*Detail from a Painting
in the Collection of Sir
Jeremiah Colman, Bt.*

COUNTRY MOODS
AND TENSES

A Non-Grammarian's Chapbook

By

EDITH OLIVIER

Chapbook, a specimen of popular literature, circulated by itinerant dealers or chapmen.

Chapman, a retail dealer at fairs, etc.
   "No tinker, pedlar, or petit chapman shall
   "wander about the towne, but such as shall
   "be licensed by two Justices of Peace."—Act
   of Parliament, Edward VI, 1553.
OXFORD ENGLISH DICTIONARY,

LONDON
B. T. BATSFORD, LTD.
15 NORTH AUDLEY STREET, W.1

BOOKS BY EDITH OLIVIER

NOVELS

THE LOVE CHILD
AS FAR AS JANE'S GRANDMOTHER'S
THE TRIUMPHANT FOOTMAN
DWARF'S BLOOD
THE SERAPHIM ROOM

BIOGRAPHY

THE ECCENTRIC LIFE OF ALEXANDER CRUDEN
MARY MAGDALEN

PERSONAL MEMOIR

WITHOUT KNOWING MR. WALKLEY

First Published September, 1941

Reprinted January, 1942

MADE AND PRINTED IN GREAT BRITAIN

FOR REGINALD PEMBROKE

MY FRIEND FROM OUR CHILDHOOD

BECAUSE HE LOVES ALL COUNTRY THINGS, AS   DO

AUTHOR'S NOTE

The Author expresses her sincere thanks to the following :

Mrs. Robert Bridges, and the Oxford University Press, for permission to quote the lines on pages 15 and 33 from the *Testament of Beauty*, by the late Poet Laureate.

Lady Newbolt, for Sir Henry Newbolt's lines on page 28, taken by permission from his book, "Poems New and Old", published by Messrs. John Murray.

Sir Edward Marsh, for his translation of La Fontaine's Fable, *Le Rat de Ville et le Rat de Champs*.

Captain T. R. Henn for reading the proofs.

Miss Rosemary Olivier for tracing a particularly elusive quotation.

ACKNOWLEDGMENT

The Publishers would like to thank the following for the photographs appearing in this book :

Mr. G. P. Abrahams, for fig. 37.

Associated Press, for figs. 4, 11.

Mr. Cecil Beaton, for figs. 10, 24, 25.

Central Press, for fig. 16.

The late Brian C. Clayton, for fig. 68.

The Daily Mirror, for figs. 32, 36, 41, 57, 62.

Mr. J. Dixon-Scott, for figs. 12, 17.

Dorien Leigh, Ltd., for figs. 3, 7, 13, 18, 19, 21, 26, 27, 28, 31, 47, 48, 51, 52, 75.

Fox Photos, for figs. 5, 35, 38, 46, 54, 55.

Leonard and Marjorie Gayton, for fig. 15.

Messrs. Gibson, Penzance, for fig. 60.

Mr. F. A. Girling, for figs. 40, 41.

Mr. Harold G. Grainger, for figs. 34, 73.

Mr. E. M. Hickmans, for figs. 23, 39, 74.

Miss M. K. Swayne-Edwards, for figs. 50, 56.

Mr. Will F. Taylor, for figs. 8, 9, 20, 22, 29, 43, 45, 59, 64, 70, 71.

The Times, for fig. 58.

Mrs. J. W. J. Underell, for figs. 14, 67, 72.

Mr. F. R. Winstone, for figs. 2, 6, 30, 33, 76, 77.

They would also like to thank Sir Jeremiah Colman, Bt., for permission to include the painting used as a frontispiece from his magnificent collection of cricketing pictures, Mr. Rex Whistler for the drawing on fig. 53, and Messrs. W. T. Spencer, of New Oxford Street, for the loan of prints from their unrivalled collection.

CONTENTS

2　Black Magic : a Scarecrow

3   White Magic : Giant Hemlock

THE GRAMMAR OF COUNTRY LIFE

The Grammar of Country Life

I NEVER LEARNT ENGLISH GRAMMAR. MY MOTHER AVERRED that it did not exist; but she considered that the Latin Grammar was a Grand Thing, so she taught us a little of that, which unfortunately I have forgotten. Now I begin to regret that my grammarless education has debarred me from the familiar use of a good many attractive and expressive words. I shall never know their legitimate meaning, but I fancy that some of these must be more nearly related to life than to school-books, and related especially to life in the country.

"Moods", for instance. Grammatically I know not what they mean; but in life who has not experienced them? For they create and re-create the world around us all. That world is for ever changing, and its changes are largely due to changes in our own moods. I expect that this is especially true of life in the country, which is more solitary than life in towns, and is therefore more susceptible of an idiosyncratic. So, let the townsman say what he will, country life has more variety than life in the town. It is racy of the soil, and varies with each village, house, and even with each individual. The personal mood has time and space in which to expand and to express itself—and it expresses itself mainly by creating its own world.

On the other hand, no one could bear to live in a town without the constant artificial stimulants provided by traffic lights, cinemas, cocktail parties, evening papers, and what they call "night life". Such things are absolutely essential to counteract the dreary sameness of life in a street; but the variety which they give is standardised. It is variety cut to a pattern, devised by someone outside ourselves, and might well be delivered with the morning milk or the afternoon post.

The INFINITIVE is pre-eminently the Country Mood. I live remote from libraries, and so am obliged to make my own collection of books of reference. Chief among these is the Oxford English Dictionary (two-volume edition to suit the capacities of

3

my purse and of my house). Here I learn that Infinitude is "the quality of being infinite; boundlessness; immensity; vastness". This is Nature's primal mood. It is so entirely the countryman's atmosphere that he is hardly aware of it, though without it he could not live. It is the air he breathes, the serene silence falling for ever on his ears. It gives to the eyes of an old countryman the aloof majesty which also appears on the faces of seamen. That look comes out of a heart at peace and at home, through familiarity with the vision of great spaces.

When a countryman lives for a time exiled in the town, the Infinitive Mood is bound to call him home sooner or later.

Thirty years ago, there lay dying in a London hospital an old dock labourer. No one knew his history, and no relations ever came to visit him. For years he had drifted about the sordid, crowded streets of Poplar and Rotherhithe, Wapping and Lime-house, where the air is acrid with an indescribable mixture of smells and stinks, odours and scents; and where the ear is deafened by a babel of sound, composed of the jargons and argots of every port in the world. This noise and these smells are any-thing but English, and yet can be found nowhere but in London —unless, perhaps, in Marseilles. The restless tides had at last washed this broken fragment of flotsam and jetsam into the quiet ward of a great London hospital, and for some time the Chaplain tried vainly to hear the words which the old man was trying to say. He seemed to be asking for something—something which he wanted desperately—something without which he could not peacefully die.

The words came through at last.

"The Marlborough Downs—in the rain."

The sought-for vision returned as he spoke. He saw his downs. A sudden smile swept over his face, as the wind sweeps across a corn-field. Then he died.

Because country people are so quietly at home in the Infinitive Mood, strangers sometimes fancy that they have nothing what-ever to do. Country Life is conceived of as one long *dolce far niente*. Nothing could be farther from the truth. The country-man possess no leisure: leisure possesses him. It holds him in its great spaces, but within those he is always busy. Country leisure is like the wide margin of a book. The argument is in the printed column, but the page's beauty depends upon the balance given by that empty border.

The countryman's busy-ness is like the busy-ness of bees, buzzing for ever among the blossoms of immemorial lime-trees. No one could think of hurry or bustle under the shade of a lime avenue, and yet the winged honey gatherer knows that the blossoms fall only too fast. His hum has an indolent sound, but his work is unceasing. The quintessentially sweet scent of the lime flowers is the first warning that the best of the summer is over. Years are long in the country: eternities sometimes; but seasons are short, and each one brings its own occupation which must be dealt with at once, or lost for the year. Each season has its own definite character. Each brings its own work, and each its own pleasureable idleness. In the long summer evenings, there is the delicious indolence of alternating between the deck chair and the water pot; while in winter, when darkness comes in with the tea, there is unbroken solitude with books and needle-work. In the country you never forget what time of the year it is.

On the other hand, in towns the seasons have been mastered by man. Spring, Summer, Autumn and Winter are blended into one uniformity. Life is the same all through the year. The day's work hardly varies, and at night there are always the same amuse-ments—theatres, concerts, cinemas, dinners and dancing. It needed a war to remind the townsman that in some seasons of the year the nights are longer and darker than in others, and that the moon only shines on half the evenings in the month.

In the country, the Infinitive Mood merges into the IMPERATIVE. This Infinitive which broods over us, giving a greatness to little things, enrols us in its "army of unalterable law". Perforce we find that we are cogs in the great wheel which Dante saw always moving equally, driven onwards by "the Love that moves the sun and the other stars". The countryman knows that he is the servant of the powers of Nature, and in that service he finds the joy of "Perfect freedom".

Even in the purely feminine avocation known as "doing the flowers", there is this intrinsic difference between town and country. In town the flowers are found in the shops and are put into the vases. Enormous roses on very long stalks appear in mid-winter. Spring flowers scent the room at Christmas time. Lilac and magnolia trees stand in ballrooms in every season of the year.

It is all easy and lightly come by. It is one of the triumphs of our civilisation.

Whereas in the country, flowers appear in the rooms as the culmination of many months of preparation for their short time of blossoming. The earth must be dug and dunged; the seeds, bulbs and the plants must be set in the beds; there is weeding and watering to do; roses must be pruned and sweet peas staked. It is a long and varying process, brightened by success and darkened by disappointment, for Nature shows us every month that she means to be the mistress, and that all our labour must wait upon her sun and rain, her frosts, her winds and her blight. We can only dig and delve; then we must bow to her Imperative Mood.

It is the same with the store cupboard, so easily filled in London by the beneficence of Messrs. Fortnum and Mason. To them it is merely a matter of indifferently turning to another shelf and with equal facility they will hand over the counter Guava Jelly, Hymettus Honey or Sloe Gin. But in the country, a May frost may put an end to all hopes of strawberry jam for the year, and a wet September can ruin the blackberry harvest. The bee keeper must be content with the honey found in the flowers which grow within range of his own bees' flight; and although the adventurous bee owner may be daring enough to try to extend that range, the experiment does not always succeed. I once attempted something of the kind myself. Our Women's Institute possessed a hive of bees, and one year after the usual June honey harvest, we decided to carry the hive on a visit to the New Forest, where a friend offered it hospitality, so that the bees could gather heather honey in the month of August. We drove the hive into Hampshire in my car and reached our destination after some rather tremendous vicissitudes. No sooner had we arrived than the bees proceeded to swarm, and they chose to swarm on the back of a donkey which happened to be grazing by the roadside, as is the custom of animals in the forest. The donkey kicked up its heels and galloped away into the distance, with our bees swarming and stinging and buzzing upon him, and with me and my friend and the old gardener panting along in pursuit. We caught the unwilling thief at last, and the gardener recaptured the swarm; but we agreed that henceforth we would give up such attempts to go one better than Nature. We would accept the honey produced by our own flowers, and if we wanted exoticisms, a postal order to Piccadilly would be the simplest means to obtain them. Nature's Imperative Mood had best be obeyed.

Not until the signposts had been removed from all the English roads did one realise how great a part is played in the country by the INDICATIVE Mood. In a sense it is true that a country house and garden create a world apart, where its owners can live more completely than in any town house; yet country people always seem to be going somewhere.

Once or twice in the week it is urgently necessary to proceed to the nearest country town to do the household shopping or to meet a train. But these personal errands are the smallest part of the compulsory business which draws the countryman from home, for most people play some part in county life. The Bench must be attended. There are meetings of all kinds—political, religious, philanthropical or connected with county sports; there are county fetes and pageants, rallies of boy scouts and girl guides, or local musical festivals. The actual sports themselves entail a lot of travelling. Meets of the hounds, cricket matches, tennis tournaments and golf are none of them held in the dining room: they all mean a journey, longer or shorter. Then there are visits to country neighbours, luncheons and garden parties, for country people are very friendly when once they have made friends, which, it must be admitted, is a question of a good many years. Best of all, there is the eternal delight of sightseeing, and no country in the world is more full of beauty than is England. So in peace time, a large part of the country dweller's time is spent on the road, and one of the chief changes brought about by the war is that all this has ended. No one has the petrol for these pursuits; and in any case no one has time or inclination for them. We are all at work. So we come to a new war-time experience. Our work takes us to places a little off the roads upon which we generally travel. We fancied we knew our neighbourhood perfectly, but now we suddenly find ourselves pulled up at a cross road, helpless for lack of a signpost. The yokel is cautious, too, about giving directions. He knows well that we are probably German parachutists.

"I bain't a-givin' 'ee any information" was the answer received by the Mother's Union speaker who innocently asked the way to the vicarage; and thus it is learnt that for the time being the Indicative Mood is banished from the countryside.

The SUBJUNCTIVE is a difficult Mood to define. The Oxford Dictionary, with much else, says it refers to "Something subjoined or dependent". It is used to "express a wish, command or exhortation", and therefore must obviously refer to conversation. It deals, then, with human relationships. The country community is a group of people linked up, "joined or dependent" one upon another in an intimacy impossible in great towns. In a village, even business connections are far from being purely "business". The local shop is still the local Club, as the town booksellers' were two hundred years ago. In the shop the stranger asks his way on his first morning in the village: he learns the easiest method of sending for goods from the railway station three miles off. He is told the name of the parson, doctor or lawyer—nay, he is introduced to these and other inhabitants of the place should they enter the shop while he is in it.

"This is the gentleman (or lady) who has taken the late Mrs. Blank's house."

The gentleman (or lady) realises that he has now become part of a social entity.

Even the postmaster and mistress are no impersonal civil servants. They are heard gladly calling to each other the news that the vicar's son has telegraphed announcing the birth of twins. And, now, in these anxious days of war, a fatal telegram is not allowed to be delivered by the usual telegraph boy, freewheeling recklessly up to the door. The postmaster himself carries it to the house and sees that it is handed to its recipient with all the consideration and sympathy which at such times becomes alive among friends.

Neighbourliness is a living force in village life. Illness or bereavement calls it out to an extraordinary extent. A working man will sit night after night at the bedside of a mate who is ill, in spite of his own hard day's work on either side of that trying vigil. I remember once going to the house of a cottage woman, to find she had gone out, leaving her washing in confusion in the kitchen. As I stood looking round, she came in out of the neighbouring cottage, saying—

"I have just been in next door to lay out Mrs. May's poor little boy who died this morning. She's only a poor creature. Couldn't so much as lay out a cat, as the sayin' is."

This was not a "sayin'" with which I had been hitherto

4   Town Flowers

5   Country Flowers

6, 7 · The Village Shop

familiar, but I welcomed it as an addition to my knowledge of phrase and fable.

"Giving lifts" has always been a country practice, but in these days people are more than ever "subjoined or dependent" upon one another for journeys from place to place. In the country, however, there is always the dear old carrier's cart, now looking like a motor-bus of greater or less dignity or capacity. But motor or not, it has not changed its character. It is still as friendly as ever. It will stop at an isolated door to collect the watercress gatherer, the occupants eagerly helping the newcomer to get her baskets aboard. And throughout the journey it resounds with a perpetual chorus of local gossip. Talk and laughter fill it, as do the smells and the cackling of the livestock which accompanies many of the passengers.

These carriers' carts are the descendants of the mediæval "Char" used in Chaucer's day. This vehicle was drawn by five horses and was covered by a gaily painted canvas hood. It was only used by women, for the men rode from place to place. I remember one such vehicle, and it must have been a last remnant of the "Merrie England" of the road. In my childhood, the ordinary village carrier drove a van with a dreary grey hood. All those vans were alike; and in Wilton we despised them, as our own carrier's cart was a brilliantly painted thing, in green and blue and red, its name printed in large letters on one side. It was called "The Matoka": I never knew why. It went to Salisbury and back every day, and was a most sociable equipage with its passengers in rows on either side and its stacks of parcels at the back.

The CONDITIONAL Mood is one of which the country is only now slowly learning the existence, for, by its very name, it suggests that conditions can change. Hitherto, in spite of motor buses and wireless sets, life in most country villages has been, outwardly at least, an unconditional denial of this. "*It always 'as been*", and "*It never 'as been*" are unanswerable arguments for and against any new proposal; and the National Anthem of the countryside has ever been—

> "As it was in the beginning, is now, and ever shall be,
> World without end."

But the war is changing the villages; and those which lie farthest from the danger zone were the first to be aware that

2

this was so. At the very outbreak of war, those people who lived
in what were known as "safe" areas learnt that, in the day when
an Englishman's house was first described as his castle, it was a
fortress not only for himself, but for anyone else in need of
shelter. So in many parts of the country every house is now full
of strangers. The sharp thin faces of townswomen and children
stand out among natives in the village streets; and every cottage
contains an " uncle" and an "auntie" to one or two evacuated
school children. There is something very touching in the sight
of these small children (each with a gas-mask slung across its
shoulders) marching to school in the morning, hand in hand
with their guides, who may be the children of the house in which
they are billeted, or the husband on his way to work, or perhaps
the mother of the family who has left her "cleaning up" to
shepherd the little flock to school.

And where there are no evacuated children there are sure to
be soldiers, or civil servants, or munition workers, who want
lodging.

The age-long peace of the village is now shattered by the roar
of aeroplanes passing on their way to bomb the nearest town,
and perhaps dropping a few bombs in country meadows to kill
one or two cows or rabbits in them. Sometimes the raider even
decides to smash the village church or the school, vainly hoping
to create a panic among the sturdy country labourers. All the
village people have joined war service squads. The men are in
the Home Guard. The women have got their First Aid certifi-
cates. No more peaceful evenings by the fireside, for it is no
longer a case of keeping the home fires burning. The duty in this
war is to keep your own fire dark and to help to extinguish your
neighbour's if an incendiary bomb should fall on his house.

And what about "TENSES"? I only know of three—PAST,
PRESENT, FUTURE; and the Present is the only one which is ever
actually in existence. It is that point upon the highway from
which one looks before and after. The Past is a long road,
vanishing into a distance veiled in rose-coloured mists. The
Future is a short lane which very soon reaches a turning beyond
which one cannot see. So a book written in the Present must draw
its material mainly from the Past.

But there are more complex tenses belonging to the more
advanced branches of grammar—the Perfect, the Imperfect and

8, 9   From Generation to Generation : the Hop Harvest

10, 11 Evacuees

the Pluperfect. Some people look on the Past as always an Imperfect tense. They think it consists only of muddy lanes, poverty-stricken hovels and insanitary smells; while in their eyes the Future is a Pluperfect paradise of tarmac roads, council houses and drains. For others, the Past is the Golden Age—all simplicity, picturesqueness and content; and the Future is a hideous prospect from which they can only avert their eyes.

Yet perhaps in the Future we shall find that, as a result of this war, the regrettable gulf between town and country, which opened in the last 150 years, will be closed again, by those piteous ambassadors from the towns, now being made welcome in the country. Friends found in time of adversity will not be lost in happier days. The rural and the urban points of view may find themselves permanently nearer each other.

Village life in itself may become more communal. Neighbours will have formed the habit of working together, and will have found that it makes for happiness and efficiency.

And what will the country of the future look like? When houses, churches and schools have been destroyed, one rather dreads the new buildings; though there is no reason why the loss of the treasures of the past should necessarily destroy that vision which once made it possible to create them.

We cannot foresee the future conditions; what we can do is to keep alive the spirit of Faith. Those who continue to believe in Goodness, Truth and Beauty, will always spread them around, in whatever conditions. The eye of Faith sees farther than the Conditional Mood.

THE FIRST MOOD

INFINITIVE

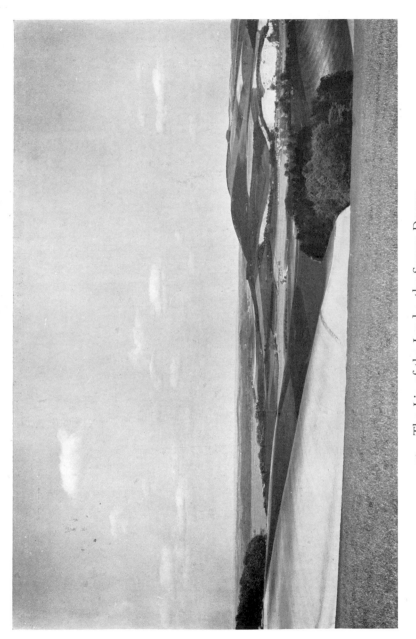

12   The Lie of the Land : the Sussex Downs

13   The Lie of the Land :   Chiltern Skyscape

1 The Lie of the Land

D R. VAUGHAN CORNISH HAS DESCRIBED HOW, ON HIS FIRST
visit to Stonehenge, he found that for a few moments he
"forgot the ancient monument". He had "turned to
view the surrounding scene . . . and was at once impressed
by the *circularity* of the horizon . . . very rarely do we find
ourselves standing thus in the middle of a *round* world. . . . Enter-
ing within the circle of Stonehenge, I looked through the open-
ings of the colonnade towards the several parts of the panorama,
and saw the circularity of the sky-line emphasised by the re-
curving foreground of the sarsen stones".

Those who are fortunate enough to have been born near
Stonehenge have always been aware of the shape of the universe.
It is one of their privileges to realise the full import of the lie
of the land. It is an experience which may have a profound effect
upon one's life. That experience led Robert Bridges to begin
his *Testament of Beauty* with the words:

> 'Twas late in my long journey, when I had clomb to where
> The path was narrowing and the company few,
> A glow of childlike wonder enthral'ed me, as if my sense
> Had come to a new birth purified, my mind enrapt
> Re-awakening to a fresh initiation of life;
> With like surprise of joy as any man may know
> Who rambling wide hath turned, resting on some hill-top
> To view the plain he has left, and see'th it now out-spredd
> Mapp'd at his feet, a landscape so by beauty estranged
> He scarce will ken familiar haunts, nor his own home,
> May-be where far it lieth, small as a faded thought.

What is it that attracts one in a panoramic view? It certainly
has a very general attraction, for one of the first pleasures offered
to a newly arrived guest is to "walk up the hill and see our view".
What is this irresistible charm? It is partly, I believe, a sense of
being let into the secret of a great architect's conception, as
though Christopher Wren had shown us the city he planned,

"standing four-square" like the heavenly Jerusalem. The mind cannot but find satisfaction in the vision of a great fulfilled conception.

A sense of the lie of the land on the grand scale must have been a feature of the earliest civilisation which left its mark on this country. It is something which to-day is beyond our range, in spite of the airy way in which we can fly from continent to continent in a few hours. It is only during this century that students are realising again that the men who built Avebury and Stonehenge saw all England as a great topographical unity.

Those who live near these great monuments have always felt a pride in them, but the archæologists of the last century had then enough to do burrowing down to the earthworks, as they tried to puzzle out their lost history and to learn something of their builders. Now, like Dr. Vaughan Cornish at Stonehenge, they are turning to scan the horizons in which are set these mysterious temples, camps and barrows. Nothing gives such a sense of the grandeur of Nature and of the human spirit than the realisation that though these earthworks are buildings made of dust, they are not merely emblems of man's mortality. They speak of his victory over Time, and are set into the great scheme of the Creator by men who had the vision to see that creation as a whole. Avebury, Stonehenge, Old Sarum, Maiden Castle, St. Catherine's Hill, Glastonbury Tor, and all the other famous ancient sites in southern England, are indeed grand places when simply viewed in themselves; but they uplift the soul when it is grasped that they are parts of a supreme plan. It is like standing upon Mount Pisgah. From that point Moses must have seen the Promised Land more clearly than did the men who blew their trumpets outside the City of Jericho. They brought the walls down, but the Seer looked beyond the wreckage and saw a new world.

There are great panoramas which have a unity apart from that created by pre-historic builders. No one conveys like Hilaire Belloc the inspiration given by the revelation of the Lie of the Land. In the *Path to Rome* he tells of his pilgrimage from Toul in Lorraine to Rome, and he says, "When I call up for myself this great march, I see it all mapped out in landscapes, each of which I caught from some mountain, and each of which joins on to that before and to that after it, till I can piece together the whole

14   The Lie of the Land : Chalk Country

15   The Lie of the Land : Village Quiet

road. . . . They unroll themselves in all their order till I can see
Europe, and Rome shining at the end''.

After that experience, a fine view must ever be something
more than a fine view.

Still, many views impress themselves upon the memory simply
as, in themselves, things of beauty. I remember the shock of
surprise with which I first looked down from that amazing
natural rampart formed by the enormous cliff of La Baume as it
rises unexpectedly from the Camargue. Below it lay miles of the
level land of Provence; and the tideless waters of the Mediterranean seemed to bound an equally tideless marshland.

One comes on another memorable view on the road from
London to Ely. I saw it first one evening. We drove out of
Stretham, when suddenly, as we went down the hill, the
cathedral broke upon our sight. It seemed to be hanging from
the sky by a jewelled chain, for curved above it that night was
the softly radiant arch of a rainbow. That memory lit the rest of
our journey.

There are fewer wide views in the Lake Country than one
would expect, because the mountains are so crowded together
that you must climb very high before being able to see far. There
is a wonderful view from the Striding Edge of Helvellyn, and the
country round Derwentwater and Ullswater is open enough to
give one the thrill of recognising the general plan of the landscape. But I think that the thing I am describing belongs more to
downs than to mountains, and that is why the architects of the
earthworks place their triumphs of building in the south country
chalklands. The camps and barrows are the natural completion
of those great curved contours.

English people are reverting to the spirit of their Neolithic
predecessors and are now beginning once more to build their
houses on the high ground. Unfortunately they have not yet
recovered the genius with which the ancient builders took their
natural surroundings into their building and were in turn absorbed by Nature into its primeval pattern. Instead of this, a
modern house placed on a skyline is nearly always an eyesore,
while it should be the culminating point where the eye finds
its resting place. This may be partly because the material of the
modern house clashes with green peace of the turf.

Nevertheless, concrete is one of the materials which could be

3

at home beside an earthwork. It, too, can take to itself a curved outline. An enormous concrete viaduct—a line of solemn arches —might without incongruity carry a modern motor road over a valley from one down summit to another, and I look forward to some day seeing one in Wiltshire. And then concrete houses might be placed nearby, but they must be built by architects who look at the lie of the land, and not by those whose happiest memories are of Grosvenor House and the Dorchester Hotel. These new architects must don the mantle of that prehistoric race who were humble enough to see their own works as small parts in Nature's great design; and who yet were proud enough to set their creations in the key positions of her noble conception.

There is, of course, much beauty in the country, apart from the wonder of the lie of the land. After the days of the Saxons, the high escarpments were left to castles and fortresses, which still proudly occupied the commanding positions from which the garrisons could watch over the peaceable inhabitants pursuing their avocations below. But the villages themselves were built beside the streams. Here were the abbeys and the cathedrals. Here were the manor houses and the country seats. Here were the farms and the cottages. In mediæval times people avoided wide views. Enclosures were their idea of peace; and for them, beauty was a shut-in thing, delicate and near the eye, like an illumination in a Missal. They bequeathed to us the love of domesticity both in house and garden; and that idea is precious still to English people. The red brick manor house, the walled garden with its roses and pæonies, the little village church, the tiny stone bridge across the stream—these mean for many people the charm of the English country. They are all combined in the word "homely". They possess a beauty filled with tenderness, and they carry with them a hundred childish memories. Yet a realisation of the far-flung majesty of the lie of the land embraces all those lesser beauties, and infinitely transcends them.

17   Country Nightfall

2 Country Nights

"WHILE THE EARTH REMAINS, SEED TIME AND HARVEST, and cold and heat, and summer and winter, and day and night shall not cease." So God said to Noah, as he and his family came out of the ark, and to the modern town-dweller such an idea is indeed archaic. He can't possibly believe it, and if he could, he doesn't want to. Our civilisation aims at obliterating the seasons and the time of day, and it has almost succeeded. The prosperous townsman eats peaches in January and strawberries all the year round. Central heating has substituted for that barbarous alternation of cold and heat a mean temperature in his house or hotel of about 70 degrees Fahr. Come summer, come winter, he finds in the cinema always the appropriate setting for the picture he has come to see. Without leaving his seat in the darkened theatre, he passes from the tornado and the earthquake to sea bathing or ice skating, and one flick will carry him from the sand-strewn desert to the flower-filled garden. The unblinking radiance of the street lamps comes between him and the sky; and it required a black-out to bring him the startling revelation of the exotic beauty of the moon.

Life in the cities has, in fact, achieved a polished sameness which has vanquished those old-fashioned seasons with their rough edges and their uncertain frontiers; it has substituted convenience for romance. This is a disaster, because although romance is far more worth-while than convenience, yet it is fatally easy to outgrow, while dependence on convenience is an all but incurable disease.

War-time evacuation has brought this home to us. Townspeople love the thought of the country. They revel in a day there. In theory, the ideal of every Englishman is a country cottage of his own, with a garden from which he will eat his own vegetables, and a pigsty from which his own pig will send him an unbroken string of sausages and unending sides of bacon. Yet, in spite of the fact that the town habit is a new thing in this country, and that hardly one-fifth of our urban population has behind it more than one generation of town dwellers, nearly one-half of the evacuees went home in two months or less. They would rather be bombed than bored.

And in some ways the country is certainly difficult to live in. In wet weather the village streets become quagmires; there is nothing to buy in the one shop, and less than nothing to look at in its window: if you want anything beyond the daily necessities, you must wait till someone goes to "town". The "privy" in the garden is nothing but revolting after the indoor "convenience"; and the dark nights are paralysing to mind and body.

As a matter of fact, however, the black-out is less black in a village than in a town. Rows of houses add their shadows to the darkness of night, while where there are only a few buildings the wide horizon holds and diffuses a faint afterglow of daylight when the sun has long set. For very few hours is the "traveller in the dark" left without either the "tiny spark" of the distant stars, the silver glory of the moon, the crimson legacy of sunset or the rosy promise of a dawning day.

But in the darkness (and still more in the black-out) towns-people know that houses are "company", street walls are guides and passers-by are welcomely human. For those who are freshly come from town, country nights are filled only with panic. A young Londoner came to a village a few years ago, as a model for a sculptor friend of mine. He resolutely refused to come to the studio after dark, saying that, if he did, "something would bogue out at him".

"There is nothing here that could possibly hurt you", we said.

"There might be a wolf", he answered.

We told him there had been no wolves in England for hundreds of years.

"Well, there are plenty of foxes", was his last card.

This could not be denied, nor could the unjustifiable panic be ended. Country nights were simply fearsome.

Yet in them is one of the never-failing joys of country life. Throughout the year, "the Heavens are telling the glory of God", and, as the fugual impulse of Haydn's fine chorus suggests, night may uniformly follow night, and yet each will differ in glory from the last, for their length and their brilliance wax and wane with the seasons, except for those who have the misfortune to live either on the Equator or in the Ritz.

It is hard to say in which time of the year country nights are the most magic, though more people know them in summer.

Perhaps in those months their chief beauty lies in their long twilight. The sun never goes very far below the horizon. He passes out of sight to make a journey which is really a long, shallow ellipse, leaving our sky free for the planets which then voyage past us "like a fleet of ships". Life holds few more exquisite experiences than those hours of on-coming dusk when one gazes into the deepening spaces of the sky to see the stars appear one by one. They say that it brings good fortune to count seven stars on seven consecutive nights, and this is not so easy as one might expect. On some nights clouds come up and spoil the sky for counting and then one has to begin all over again; but to me, it is good fortune even to look for those seven stars. Staring after them into the heavens, one passes into a state of ecstasy in which it seems possible to see any celestial vision. But summer evenings have other pleasures nearer to earth. After sunset, there begin to float about the garden many demurely coloured moths who move soundlessly among the flower beds, but more often about the wood, for they love trees. Bats flit feverishly about, darting erratically hither and thither with their tiny shrill cries, inaudible to anyone over forty years old. Water fowl come home to the stream, taking to the water with a long splash and calling each other in tones of hoarse beauty. Other night birds wake in the meadows. Several warblers have songs which one often mistakes for the nightingale; but when that divine voice does at last break upon the darkness, there is no longer any doubt. No one says, "Is that the nightingale?" Instead, the whisper is "There he is"; and people always do whisper, lest the magic singer should be frightened away; but this is quite a mistake, as the nightingale loves noise. When we were children, we used to walk out to hear him where he sang in a hawthorn hedge between the high road and the railway. Sometimes he refused to sing, as he often does, being as capricious as other virtuosi; but if the train came puffing and roaring along the line, the nightingale burst at once into his loveliest song. He tried to outsing the engine.

Perhaps scents are the most subtle of all the pleasures of summer evenings. As the flowers vanish in the dusk they return to the air in fragrance, thus finding their way to the most spiritual of the senses. Honeysuckle, mignonette, wallflowers, tobacco plants, roses, lilies and jessamine breathe again from their invisible beds. There is the pungent smell of a small herb trodden underfoot; or in the dark avenue, the scent of the lime blossoms becomes intoxicating. No sound of distant church bells over the meadows has a greater power to evoke the memories of childhood than have these sweet faint garden scents.

Autumn nights begin with harvests and harvest homes, and they bring their own scents too. These are homely workaday smells—the smell of dead leaves swept up and burnt, or that smell of burning weeds which carries behind it a long lazy trail of blue smoke, its colour fading and its scent strengthening as night falls. Autumn evenings are filled with country activities. Bell-ringers practise for Christmas, and boys shout in the street, pushing Guy Fawkes on an old barrow. They let off squibs and send bonfires blazing skywards. In Honiton on the fifth of November they used to roll burning tar barrels down the steep village street, with a startling effect of wild and primitive gaiety. In early autumn, some of the most famous country fairs take place; and they, too, fill the air with the light of oil flares, and the ugly stimulating music of merry-go-rounds. In autumn evenings, the stars come out more quickly than they could do in the lingering summer dusk. In fact there are nights when you can't see the sky for the stars. Then there sweep up the famous November fogs, very different things in the country to the yellow, soot-laden, eye-irritating stuff to be met with in London. These country fogs are white and wispy. They gather in the hollows and float about on the high ground; but only rarely are they thick enough to prevent a star here and there from breaking through.

As the autumn deepens, country evenings become indoor affairs. The sportsmen are "home from the hills", bringing the smell of corduroy and wet leaves; and family parties gather round the fire to roast the little English chestnuts which have fallen from the trees—too small to be really worth roasting, and yet too sweet to be left outside. The difference between English and Spanish chestnuts is very like the difference between country and town. The town chestnut is a more important thing; but the country product is more fun. In my childhood, we ate English truffles too, and no one can deny that these equal, or even excel, the truffles of Perigord. But in my part of the world, at least, the truffle dog is now an extinct breed, and as we haven't yet trained pigs to forage for us, that autumn delicacy must remain a memory. But even without truffles, autumn in the country is

18   Country Moonlight

19, 20   Gipsy Meals

the season for feasting, and all over England people can live on the country round. Venison, grouse, wild duck, partridges, pheasants, snipe, woodcock, hares and rabbits—all fall into the pot ; and squires and keepers, beaters and poachers, gypsies and squatters dip into it while the stars burn on in the autumn night.

Winter nights have a wild clear beauty. Stars glitter through the frosty air, and the snow on the ground shines almost as brightly as the moon. Village people are well aware of the fact that there are light evenings during only half of each month. They stay indoors on dark nights, and fix their club dinners and other entertainments for the week of the full moon. During the dark fortnight you can nowadays hear the wireless from most houses as you go down the village street. Father sits at home, listening, with his pipe in his mouth: the elder son manages to find his way to the pub.; while mother mends and darns as she does all through the year, though she says that in winter she seems to have more time for it. Nowadays, no church bells ring the old year out. We must wait till the end of the war before we hear again that lovely clanging cadence. Then I hope the sirens will have ceased to sound, for no one surely will wish in future to herald a new year with that plaint so laden with woeful associations.

Spring nights are shortened at each end by the miracle of bird song. As February advances the evenings sparkle with the wet whiteness of myriads of snowdrops in the grass, and, overhead, the clear separate notes of thrushes and blackbirds which fall with a clarity like snowdrops too. The sheep begin to wear their bells again, and as they wear them the chords ring out which the shepherd has been collecting year by year at many fairs. He judges, criticises and improves his carillon till the harmony reaches his ideal. Later in the spring the climax of the bird song is in the early morning. The first birds wake the sun. They call him out of bed, and as he slowly and grandly comes up the sky the whole chorus bursts out to meet him. Individual songs are lost. The air is full of a tangle of sound, which somehow preserves a celestial harmony.

Across the happy variety of these country nights the Nazi foe has thrown his totalitarian blight of sameness. A black-out is the true emblem of the Nazi onslaught. It substitutes for Nature's ringing of the changes the dull roar of aeroplanes overhead: the autumn weed burning and the Guy Fawkes bonfires must give place to the horrid glare of fires destroying homes, churches and hospitals. No more may the cowman go from shed to shed carrying his hurricane lamp from which there shines a tallow candle. The lantern might call down a Hun. Instead he must keep an electric torch in his pocket till he enters the byre, and then must tend the mother and her calf by its light, which he has carefully shaded with "at least two layers of paper". Country roads have suddenly become dangerous for walkers. Village people seem unable to believe that the motor driver cannot see an unlighted figure on the road. Bicyclists have been forced to learn this by fines, but the foot passenger has not yet realised that he now forms part of a stream of traffic, and so he must conform to the traffic laws. He still thinks that all the world knows that he is Jim Jones going home at his usual hour—an hour which is naturally known to all his neighbours; and the faintly lit car from the outer world makes no impression upon him till it has him under its wheels.

So the dark nights pass—dark with a new inhuman darkness although it is made by man. Morning comes slowly, for a perpetual "summer time" has carried the night an hour forward. A few figures grope their way down the dark street towards the church, where the early Communion takes place in almost complete darkness. The great church near my home has a new beauty and holiness at this early hour. Above the High Altar the apse soars full 70 feet over the Sanctuary into the roof. The great high building is still lost in darkness at eight o'clock in the morning. The worshippers grope their way to their seats by the light of three veiled lamps. The two candles on the altar seem a very long way off. They touch the figure of the priest, and then, by some kind of miracle, they throw their tiny gleam sheer up into the apse upon which there is a colossal mosaic figure of the Lord in Glory. The faint light does not illuminate His Face, which remains in shadow, but it touches the tesseræ of broken gold behind it, creating a large and vaguely outlined nimbus.

There is great beauty in this unexpected effect and also there is a world of romance. But, still more, there is the reminder that above the horror of a new heathendom the beauty of holiness remains untouched; and the shadows in the church cannot reach the glory which surrounds the Head of Christ.

21 Summer on the Pond

22 Winter on the Pond

23, 24 Early Summer

THE SECOND MOOD

IMPERATIVE

1 The Weather

Whether the weather be cold,
  Or whether the weather be hot,
We have to weather the weather
  Whether we like it or not.

THOSE WORDS WERE WOVEN ROUND THE BORDER OF A carpet made in the Wilton carpet factory early in the last century. They express a part of the countryman's attitude towards the weather, but there is more to be said about it than that. He accepts what is sent without rebellion, treating the weather as he treats all forces of Nature; but he knows that this force must not only be accepted: it must also be studied.

Two girls, who worked under me in the Women's Land Army during the last war, made great friends with the labourers on the farm. They told me that while the men were at work they were never silent. They talked all day. I asked what they talked about.

"Always the same thing. The weather."

In the social life of towns, talking of the weather indicates a cowardly collapse into the slough of despond. It suggests that the talkers can find no subject in common, so they tacitly agree to fill the minutes they must spend in each other's company with something in which neither pretends to take the smallest interest.

But in the country, everything depends upon the weather; it means the countryman's living: his occupations subject him every day to its vagaries: his sports and pleasures are made or marred by it. The weather must always be to him a subject of supreme interest and importance.

The very clothes worn in the country proclaim this, for they must be, first and last, weatherproof. This is the one thing which the rich townsman or woman knows about the country before setting foot in it. The woman appears on the first morning in a disguise betraying openly her natural doubt and her unconquerable fear of what the weather will do next. A tough Harris tweed, gingerbread in colour, and smelling strongly of the bogs from which it originally issued, firmly grips the body, kept to the waist by a stiff leathern belt. Over this is worn a Burbery over-coat, colour rather pale mud; and both these garments are riddled with pockets enough to carry a day's rations, in case the party should be marooned in some completely barbarous and inaccessible stretch of country. Thick woollen stockings, knitted in that "useful" cable pattern which imparts a psychological fortitude to the legs, terminate in wonderful high boots, warmly lined within, and crêpe soled without. Tremendous and expen-sive gauntlet gloves conceal the elegant natural shape of the beautifully manicured hands; and the head is bound in a gaily coloured handkerchief, protected in its turn by a mackintosh peaked hood.

Ordinary country people, though their clothes are not so expensive, are also never very far from their mackintoshes, and they often carry an umbrella; while the country labourer hangs a sack over his shoulders and fastens a strap round the legs of his trousers a little way below the knee. This latter, however, is to protect from adders as much as from wet. Once well protected no weather is so bad when you are in it as it seems to be when you look at it through the window. Sir Henry Newbolt was right when he sang:

> Caught in a copse without defence
> Low we crouched to the rain-squall dense;
> Sure, if misery man can vex,
> There it beat on our bended necks.
>
> Yet when again we wander on
> Suddenly all that gloom is gone:
> Under and over and through the wood,
> Life is astir and life is good.
>
> Well is it seen that every one
> Laughs at the rain and loves the sun.

But when the labourers talk all day of the weather, their view is practical rather than poetic. Every activity in the country is rooted in the weather; and the agriculturalist or gardener watches the weather portents as carefully as the stockbroker studies the international money market, or the racing man the form of horses. The countryman's weather knowledge is direct and first-hand. It is also generally reliable, although a logician would probably not agree that his conclusions were legitimately derived from his premises. But even in pre-war days, when the wireless kindly forewarned us every evening of the approaching weather, the wise farmer generally cut off before that piece of information. He preferred his own forecast. The science of meteorology is not, so far, an exact one, and labourers have not been surpassed as prophets. They still can discern the face of the sky, as the old roadmender does who works outside my gate. One day he confidently (and correctly) declared that the weather would not change "till thik there coach and horses do turn round and come back".

I anxiously inquired when Charles' wain would perform this manœuvre, and I learnt that it would be "not afore a month or more".

He was right as usual. In every part of the country there are points of vantage from which the natives know that because a certain distant object has suddenly come into view the weather is "on the work", and will now be wet (or fine) for a specified length of time.

Many people other than farm labourers know that if the wind changes after dawn, following the course of the sun, the day will be fine; while the wind "backing" is a sign of bad weather— wind and rain. Most people, however, fancy that the secret of the morning mist can be read equally easily, and they think that a misty morning must mean a fine day. The countryman knows better. He knows that there are mists and mists. When the mist rises suddenly, leaving a clear space near the ground, the rain is sure to come down almost at once, while a slowly dispersing mist means a beautiful day to follow. This is true at all times in the year, but especially in September, when morning mists are so common in water meadows.

Dorothy Wordsworth's description of a foggy spring morning suggests no weather forecast, but it has the beauty which belongs to her close and loving observation of all in Nature. She says:

"A thick fog obscured the distant prospect entirely, but the shapes of the nearer trees and the dome of the wood dimly seen and dilated. It cleared away between ten and eleven. The shapes of the mist, slowly moving along, exquisitely beautiful, passing over the sheep. They almost seemed to have more of life than those quiet creatures. The unseen birds singing in the mist."

That last touch is peculiarly typical of Dorothy's sensitive genius.

There are many forecasts as to days which are fateful for future weather. Everyone knows about St. Swithin, but the jingle about Candlemas Day is not so universally known.

> If Candlemas Day be fair and bright,
> Winter will have another flight:
> If Candlemas Day be dull and dour,
> Winter has gone to return no more.

And where the wind is on March 21st, there it will stay for another six weeks.

Some weather portents can only be recognised by a trained ear. Before a storm, there may sometimes be heard, high up in the trees, a short, sharp movement of wind, which flutters the trees into a curious succession of distinct taps. The men say, "the wind do blow 'oller", and they know that the strange sound is always followed by violent rain.

After a long drought the birds sometimes lose patience. They feel they can bear it no longer, and they have their own way of deceiving the worms who have stayed so long underground. They imitate the noise of falling raindrops by tapping on the earth with their bills. This trick is sometimes successful, and the worms thrust their heads through the ground, to be at once gobbled up by the cunning sportsmen.

Birds and animals have many habits which indicate the coming weather to a wise watcher. If the partridges are still flying in coveys on February 1st, it foretells a late spring; if they pair as early as the last week of January, the season will be an early one. Pheasants crow in the night to warn of the approach of bad weather, but lately they have decided that German bombs are as bad as tornadoes. They are extremely sensitive to the sound of a coming raid, and can hear, or feel, the fall of a high-explosive bomb quite twenty miles away. Then at once they lift up their voices in shrill chorus.

Cows are great weather prophets. "When my old cow do swing 'er tail like she'm doing this marnin', we'm bound to 'ave a starm afore night", said the old cowman to me; and as he drives his cows into the field early in the morning he always knows if the weather is threatening or not. If it is, they stay huddled together in a group near the gate. On the other hand, when they know that it is going to be fine, they stroll leisurely right away across the pasture, to moon about in the neighbour-hood of the farthest hedge.

In Westmorland, the cows lie on the ground when it is going to rain, and the farm men say that this is in order to keep them-selves a dry spot on the grass to rest on later in the day.

Cats have curious weather tricks, but they are such capricious beasts that you have to know your cat before you can believe it. If a cat washes nothing but her face it means that it is going to be fine; but if she carries her paw back over her ears, bad weather is coming.

I here use the word "bad" in the sense in which it is used by those of us who want to play out of doors. The worker on the land only asks that it shall be seasonable, for then it will suit his crops. He welcomes equally a peck of dust in March, a sharp April shower and the bright sun of May, as long as they do not step over into each other's domains. The weather, like the rest of the world, should keep in its place.

2   Birds and Beasts and Insects

IF A CENSUS COULD BE TAKEN, IT WOULD BE FOUND THAT THE human population of the country is terrifyingly outnumbered by the birds and beasts and insects. Humanly speaking, the population of villages is very small indeed; but around this little and diminishing, though self-important race, numberless birds, beasts and insects live their lives, pursue their ends, enchant us with their songs, annoy us by their stings and attract us to the chase.

When a London visitor arrives in a country garden, the first thing he says is nearly always, " How quiet it is". Yet it is only in the depths of winter that there is ever complete silence in the country. And then only for short intervals. A concert is always in progress, and Pan is an inexorable conductor. His music is so continuous that to an ear accustomed to the unco-ordinated clashes and bangs of the mechanised world of towns, this eternal succession of melting sounds is so peaceful that it seems to be no sound at all.

Some notes detach themselves from the perpetual flow. The bold song of a robin cuts clear against the white stillness of the snow. A startled pheasant crows harshly in the night, or a cow moans for a calf which was taken to market on the previous day. But except for these episodic notes, the visitor from the great world revels in the quiet of the country, and he only gradually learns that this precious silence is composed of living sounds.

The main reason why country noises combine to create the country quiet is that the whole of nature responds unfailingly to the conductor's baton. The music of the year follows a pre-ordained programme, and it is a lovely thing to listen for this, as one by one the separate items follow each other in a perfectly planned sequence.

The first thrushes sing while the robin is still master of the music. Their strong clear notes begin before the new year, and then slowly the chorus gathers. The birds conscientiously keep St. Valentine's Day, and after their mating, their nuptial songs gradually mount up to the full symphonies of late spring. There is nothing in Nature to equal the joyousness which fills the hours between three and five on a May morning, and these harmonies seem to be quite fortuitous. Birds are the most independent of beings. Each goes his own way, apparently with no attempt at composing a harmony. That is Pan's part. The singers merely obey the baton. And they appear with complete punctuality to throw their separate motifs into the orchestra. The migrants arrive in the New Forest with a regularity rivalling the Atlantic Clipper. Punctual as a roundabout, the Wiltshire cuckoo arrives at Downton Fair, to support the local superstition that he has been asleep under the hurdle stacks all the winter and was released by the men when they prepared for the Fair. The night-ingale arrives in my part of the world in the last days of April, though Cowper declares he once heard one on New Year's Day. Sometimes the weather checks his song on his first few nights in this country, but whenever he begins to sing, he flies away at his appointed time, abandoning the evenings to the corncrake and the nightjar. And so the birds' chorus closes down, and what is called the midsummer silence falls upon the country. But this is no silence at all. As the birds end their songs, the insects begin.

27   Rabbits on the Alert

28   A Red Squirrel's Mealtime

Already there has been a night in May when a sudden rush of clumsy and sticky cockchafers has bumped through the night colliding with everything in their path. Now the bees fill the lime avenues with their long sustained chord, and the air is full of the hum of nameless insects. Mosquitoes tune their shrill little violins. Wasps moan on their violas, to the pizzicato accompaniment of thousands of grasshoppers. In the late summer the ring doves never cease to coo, and as the autumn grows, the water birds cry and the foxes bark, while from the kennels comes the musical response of the hounds.

This harmonious unity which completes itself in the circle of the year, comes from Nature's obedience to those laws which she cannot know, but instinctively obeys. Wild birds and animals appear to be completely free. Hares play in circles and hold their boxing matches in the spring. Squirrels run along the boughs of the trees to peep saucily round the trunks, just as the whim takes them. Swallows dart along the stream, swooping down upon the invisible insects which are playing spontaneous and erratic games just above the water level. Flights of swans swing over the wide spaces of sky, filling the air with the heavy rhythmic thud of their wings. Ducks and drakes swoop down on to the river in a swift and shallow glide which leaves a long, gleaming wash behind them. All of these seem to be gaily wilful, and yet the longer one watches the birds and beasts and insects, the more one understands that theirs is the Imperative Mood. As Robert Bridges wrote:

> Ther is a young black ousel, now building her nest
> Under the rosemary on the wall . . .
>
> Could we discourse together, and were I to ask for-why
> She is making such pother with thatt rubbishy straw,
> Her answer would be surely: "I know not, but I MUST".

The Imperative is then the natural mood of the animal world; and the reason why one's friends' pet animals are often such unmitigated bores is that they have been taken out of this mood to which they belong. Animals prefer the Imperative, and owners of pets should understand this. It is a mistake to imagine that all country dwellers must possess a dog or two. Many country houses are too small to contain them, or to give the animals the illusion that they can roam about freely as if in the open air. The little villas with garden gates opening upon the main road merely give the unfortunate animals a false appearance of liberty which is only too likely to end under the wheels of a lorry. There is a widespread superstition that all Englishmen and women naturally understand dogs, but this is quite a fallacy. The gift for dog-management is a rare one, handed down for generations in some families, and never learnt at all in others. No one without it should think of owning a dog.

Keepers possess this gift, and shepherds. But then their dogs are given genuine canine careers. They have their responsible positions in the world. They carry out their duties under a discipline which they understand, and which they in turn know how to exercise. This is a fine life; and no one can say that of the life of a dog which lives in its basket, is exercised on a chain, and runs into the garden for ten minutes every evening before its owner goes to bed.

Of recent years the trend of English life (and, indeed, life in most countries) seems to be moving away from the world in which dogs can find a natural place. When I was a child I never saw a dog being taken for a walk on a chain. Now you seldom see a dog off one. No wonder they often bark and yap. Foxes bark at night, and that sound is full of the romance of a witch-haunted world, but a captive dog has no beauty in his voice: he has lost his inheritance.

Blake, whose love for animals was profoundly imaginative, knew that prison is the one curse from which they should be saved.

> A robin redbreast in a cage
> Puts all Heaven in a rage.
> A dove-house filled with doves and pigeons
> Shudders hell through all its regions.
> A dog starved at his master's gate
> Predicts the ruin of the State.
> A horse misused upon the road
> Calls to Heaven for human blood.
> Each outcry of the hunted hare
> A fibre from the brain does tear.
> A skylark wounded in the wing
> A cherubim does cease to sing.
> The game-cock clipt and arm'd for fight
> Does the rising sun affright.
> Every wolf's and lion's howl
> Raises from hell a human soul.

The wild deer, wandering here and there,
Keeps the human soul from care.
The bleat, the bark, bellow and roar
Are waves that beat on Heaven's shore.
The emmet's inch and eagle's mile
Make lame philosophy to smile.

If I was not afraid of being accused of impiety, I should like to add to these another couplet. This may be considered to be what Chaucer called "Rym dogerel", but it will be none the less appropriate for that. Here it is:

A puppy dog upon a chain
Fills all the Angel Host with pain.

The farmers' flocks and herds appear to fit into Nature's plan in spite of their captive condition. This is because, although removed from the laws of their wild state, they have submitted to a new Imperative. Their lives are adapted to another freedom, within bounds so wide that they are not observed.

There is complete peace in living on a dairy farm, and watching the cows move across the fields in the morning after milking. They seem to be unaware of the meadow palings, which nevertheless confine them. They stroll; they graze; they lie down; they chew the cud; they act as if they know they are part of the plan of the Universe.

It is the same with a flock of sheep. Sometimes, when sitting in a quiet country spot, the stillness of the day becomes remotely vocal. For a while the sounds—if sounds they be—are so distant that they cannot be picked out from the silence around. Slowly they come nearer. They form themselves into a wide, confused indefinite murmur which gradually becomes the bleating of a flock of sheep upon the road. They approach in a mounting crescendo; and as they get near it is revealed that the musicians are playing a concerto with the sheep-dog in the solo part, for now his anthoritative bark asserts itself, dominating the chorus. The flock has arrived. The sheep's voices rise as near to fortissimo as is possible while they pass: then they move away—diminuendo —into the distance, there slowly to die altogether.

29　Sheep on the Road

30　The Drover and his Dog

31   Harvest Interlude

THE THIRD MOOD

INDICATIVE

1 Road-Books and Milestones

THE INDICATIVE IS AN ESSENTIAL MOOD IN THE COUNTRY, where travellers are for ever asking the way. It is, however, a Mood possessing distinct tenses, and its Past, Present and Future are very different. Until about 1850, the main indicators were road-books and milestones. Then came a period of signposts, signal boxes, and again road-books. And the Present holds no road indicators at all. This matters less than might be expected, for people are travelling less, and as so few contemporary journeys are being made, this study of the Indicative Mood in the country shall begin in the Past.

In the Middle Ages, the traveller in Europe (or even in England if he went beyond his own county) had to be an adventurous fellow indeed. Morrison, who published one of the earliest road-books, tells his readers that they should certainly make their wills before leaving home; and one of his first bits of practical advice is an instruction on the different technique of duelling in each European country. He tells the traveller that he will meet with more thieves in England than anywhere else; but he adds this encouraging postscript: "Having taken purses by the Highway, they seldom or never kill those they rob. All private men pursue them from village to village with hue and cry".

Before the days of the Tudors there was no organised public travel in this country. Men going from one part of England to another had to rely on their own feet or on those of their beasts; and they must find their own way. Journeys were purely utilitarian, undertaken either for purposes of trade, or on pilgrimage, or on family business. The early road-books traced the course of long roads traversing the country from end to end. They indicated the whereabouts of good inns, noticed the dates of fairs and market days; and, for the benefit of those who were visiting friends in distant counties, they also gave the names of the owners of country seats on either side of the road. This last

has given an unexpected value to these early road-books. As they
went through many editions, and were published and re-
published over periods which included some centuries, they are
often the only means of tracing the successive owners of the
smaller country houses in many a county.

Leland's, first published in 1535, is the earliest extant road-
book. The writer had travelled personally on every road he
described and his book is full of vivid individual touches. Riding
out of Banbury he remembers that, as he passed the Castle, he
saw "In the Utter, a terrible prison for Convict men"; while
two centuries before the Woods replanned the city, Bath must
have been romantic rather than classical. Leland specially remembers the church built by the physician John of Tours. "He
was buried in the Presbyterie thereof, whose image I saw lying
there, at which time all the church he made lay to waste, and
weeds grew about this John of Tours' Sepulchre."

It was the later Tudors who instituted the system of posts—an
organised service of King's Messengers riding swiftly about the
country, bearing Royal Proclamations and other official documents. At distances which varied from 10 to 20 miles, there
was a post office, where the messenger left his mount and
acquired a fresh one. This secured a speed which 300 years ago
was considered magic. After a time the posts were used for the
passage of other than official letters and soon the whole service
was thrown open to private travellers. They left home on their
own horses and exchanged them at the first post for those
provided. A century later there was a fresh advance in the
organisation. Post-chaises and mail coaches appeared, and these
made it possible for family parties to travel together. From that
time onwards there appeared a succession of guide books,
written for the benefit of people who now began to travel for
pleasure—to enjoy the beauties of the country, and to visit its
great houses or its provincial centres.

These guides are, of course, now useless for their original
purpose; but they still make the most lively and reliable guides
for anyone who wishes to make a journey into the manners and
customs of those remote, urbane and deliberate days. Their
heyday was between 1750 and 1830, for by then enough
people were travelling to create a demand; and yet travel was
not so general as to make a class of cosmopolitan travellers who

32　Gipsy Life

33　Frome Market

had been about so much that they knew what to expect, and who were too blasé to be surprised by the manners of other men. Nor had enough people begun to travel to impose upon society everywhere a general standard of social etiquette. So though these guides began by showing the way to reach a place, their most important vocation was to instruct the visitor as to his behaviour after his arrival. This is what makes them so amusing to-day.

I have a small collection of these old guides, the earliest of which is *Les Délices de la Grande Bretagne*, published in 1707 for the benefit of travellers from France. It is in seven small and portable leather-bound volumes, and is illustrated by charming steel engravings—buildings, garden plans, academic dresses and so on. It is dedicated to Queen Anne; "as to whom could be offered more fitly the delights of Great Britain and Ireland than to your Majesty, herself the first and chief of the delights of this flourishing kingdom". Among the other and lesser delights are Oxford and Cambridge Dons, and all the members of both Houses of Parliament.

We all know the look of a modern station bookstall with its motley collection of coloured paper-bound books and magazines, to while away the tedium of a railway journey in these days of universal education. In the *Guide des etrangers en faisant le tour des villes de Londres et de Westminster*, published in 1763, a page of advertisements tells us what was considered likely to be the popular reading for the travellers of the day.

These are some of the books which absorbed the attention of ladies and gentlemen in the early years of George the Third's reign, as they drove about the country in their post-chaises:

The Matrimonial Preceptor.

The Whole Duty of Prayer (necessary for all Families).

The Complete Tything Table (proper for all Vestries, Clergymen and Gentlemen's Halls).

A Vindication of Providence, in which the Passions are considered in a new light.

The Court and City Register, containing Lists of both Houses of Parl't, Royal Households, Foreign Kings and Princes, Army and Navy Lists, Lord Mayor, Alderman, and Common Council. 2/9 with Almanack, 2/- without.

Moral Tales, or Dreams of Men Awake. 5/-.

6*

The Genuine Trial at Bar between James Angelsey, Esq.,
   Plaintiff, and the Rt. Hon'ble Richard Earl of Angelsey,
   for that title and estate. 5/-.
Travels through England, giving an account of all the
   Curiosities in a concise manner. By Mr. Thomas Thumb.
   1/6.
History of England with prints of the Kings in Armour. 2/6.
Milton's Essay on Education. 6d.
Acalou and Zirphile, an entertaining French Novel. 1/-.
Thoughts on Dreaming. 1/6.

The Vindication of Providence sounds rather an arid topic to
occupy the hours of a long journey; but it is given piquancy by
the new light which it promises to throw on the passions; and
the case between Lord Angelsey and his kinsman must have had
a more topical interest for the English aristocrat than the most
entertaining French novel. The Matrimonial Preceptor and the
Moral Tales could either be taken seriously or with a tongue in
the cheek; and the Court and City Register would find its place
as a bedside book when the journey was over. The prices are
surprisingly low for a time when all the printing was hand
printing, and when the editions could not have been large.

Travelling in the eighteenth century was not really expensive.
A post-horse cost 3d. a mile, but the traveller was obliged to
hire two, one for the man who came in charge, and this man
expected a tip at the end of his stage, which might be anything
from ten to twenty miles. A post-chaise cost 9d. a mile, and a
coach could be hired at the surprisingly low rate of ten shillings
a day, or 1/6 for the first hour and a shilling afterwards. If hired
by distance the charge was $1\frac{1}{2}$ miles for a shilling. Turnpike fees
were 1d. per horseman, and 6d. for a coach and six. "The prices
are for going and coming back the same day, a ticket being given
for that purpose, which you must never fail of taking." If a
London coachman, chairman or waterman was found over-
charging he was fined 40/-, half of which went to the poor-box
and half to the informer—an incentive for blackmail.

Towards the end of the century it became fashionable to make
day tours in various parts of the country. Travellers might drive
in a day through the Lake Country or the Isle of Thanet, and
guides were provided for these journeys. Passengers who toured
round the Isle of Wight learnt many little details about the

owners of the houses which they passed on the way. There was "Fairy Hill", for instance, "the delightful abode of Mrs. Glyn, sister of Sir William Oglander"; and another quiet residence was the "Priory", the property of Mr. Answell, "who married the daughter of a late proprietor". After these demure county homes, "Sundown Cottage" came as a shock. This was said to be "the villakyn of the late Mr. Wilkes", an eccentric figure who antagonised his country neighbours by wearing his London clothes in the Island. "The bag, the blue and gold, or the full dress of scarlet were his constant and unalterable drapery." Though his hospitality and benevolence were admitted, "the obliquity of his politics, the licentiousness of his private life and the abominable profligacy of his publications were the very opposite of chaste simplicity. Everything was overdone and gawdy": but this licentious creature, by the end of his life, considered himself "a volcano burnt out", so that he became a warning, rather than a danger to the young people on the Island.

Before the days of railways, there were in England many small provincial "seasons", which for the smaller fry were as important as the London one. That had always been pre-eminent, because it coincided with the Parliamentary Session, when members of both houses were obliged to be in London. They brought their wives and families with them and presented them at Court. The lesser country gentlemen were content with a Season nearer home, where the balls, assemblies and theatres were often quite as good as those in London, and where they kept in touch with their magisterial duties and continued their country sports. Town and country were thus more interlocked than is possible in these days when cities have grown so enormously, and the earlier system must have been humanising for both parties.

The *Guide des Etrangers* becomes lyrical over Newmarket. "One knows not which to admire most", says the writer, "the swiftness of the horses or the earnestness of the several spectators who lay great wagers on their favourite beasts . . . the racers fly over the plain as if they either touched not or felt not the ground they run upon. No sight except that of a victorious army in pursuit of its enemy can exceed this. Such is the swiftness and fire of an English racehorse that no horse of any country in the universe can keep pace and breath with him, running four measured miles in eight or nine minutes, sometimes less. Thus a run by such horses continuing from thence to Constantinople (which is about 2,000 miles) would be made in about 66 hours."

Eighteenth-century Bath is well known from countless memoirs and letters, but the guides often give forgotten details —details which complete the picture of the life there. Take for instance this account of a morning's bathing:

"In the morning, you are attended in a close chair, in your bathing clothes, to the Gross Bath. There the music plays while you enter the bath, and the persons that attend you present you with a little floating dish, in which is put a handkerchief, a nosegay, and of late the snuff box is added. Here the ladies and gentlemen keep to some distance, each to their proper side; but the place is but narrow, and they converse freely. Having thus amused themselves for an hour or two, they call their chairs and return to their lodgings."

When sea bathing became fashionable, the rise of seaside watering places turned what had been remote villages into new social centres. The *Thanet Itinerary* says that "the wealthy thousands from the vast metropolis hastened to the sea coast of Thanet, in order that they might refresh their weary bodies, and reinvigorate their constitutions by laving in the crystal waters of the Northern Ocean". This sparkling vision of the North Sea is very different from Mme de Noailles' impression of it a hundred years later:

"La Mer du Nord, cette mer glaciale qui a la couleur et la rage de l'hyène; qui envoie lentement, sur la côte, sa vague grise, couchée, creusée comme la Mort."

On most days in the year Mme de Noailles' hyæna-colour is more like the North Sea we know; and perhaps the *Thanet Itinerary* detected *couleur de rose* where more ordinary people would only see *couleur d'hyène*. So this account of the Assembly Rooms may also be taken with a grain of salt:

"Margate Assembly Rooms are perhaps superior to any in England. The ballroom is 87 by 45 feet, and decorated with stucco festoons, mirrors and girandoles, and five richly-cut chandeliers. Battison's Library is a most superb structure, an excellent shop and library with a spacious dome, giving light and ornament to the whole structure, from the centre of which is suspended a beautiful glass chandelier. A range of Corinthian

34   Village Gossip

35, 36   Old-Age Pensioners

columns separates the shop from the library. Busts of the poets stand on the cornices of the book-cases, and the chimney-pieces are decorated with the Muses in bas relief."

Lady bathers in Margate preferred the "enclosed bath" as they considered this to be safer; but the gentlemen were brave enough to go right into the sea. They were conveyed in "a bathing machine, concealed by a canvas umbrella, invented by one Beale, a quaker of the town". The charge for a gentleman bathing alone was a shilling, but "with a guide, 1/3d."

Margate was one of the first places to make a fashion of donkey riding, a seaside amusement which now is only enjoyed by children. But in the days of George the Third it was looked upon as an excellent opportunity for flirtation. The guide tells us that "Bennet's was then the principal Assinary. Ladies chiefly encourage it for the exercise, and for the sake of the frolic; but they are generally accompanied on these excursions by their male friends".

In none of these fashionable country towns was society better organised than it was at Tunbridge Wells, where Beau Nash was Master of the Ceremonies for some years before he went to Bath, and where his rules remained in force for nearly 100 years. If you followed the best guides you knew exactly what to do from the moment you set foot in the place, and you quickly became as completely at ease as if you were in your own club. When he arrived, the visitor was instructed to go to the Wells to "test the waters" and if he liked them he paid his "Welcome Penny" which made him free of the Wells until he left. He also must subscribe to the Assembly Rooms (5/-) and to the band. Ink, pens and paper were supplied at the Coffee House, and everybody met at the booksellers' to buy, borrow and talk about books. Life in Tunbridge Wells was very regular. People got up very early, and between seven and eight they met at the Wells to drink the waters, after which came two hours' walk. It was equally fashionable to breakfast at home or in the public rooms and gardens, where the band played under the trees. It was the correct thing to attend chapel at ten, and then the visitors scattered to amuse themselves. The band continued to play in the gardens, and people rode, walked and shopped; while on the common could be seen "pedestrians, equestrians and assinarians of all ranks, sexes and ages". In the jewellers' and toyshops there were little raffles which were considered very amusing, and in the booksellers' shops "the company met to collect the harmless satire or the panagyrics of the day". After the early dinner morning dress was discarded and everyone "appeared in full and splendid attire to see and to be seen". The Great Room was now given up to cards, and tea drinking went on in the gardens outside. Balls and theatres began at seven, a box at the play only costing 5/-, and the Beau insisted on rigid punctuality at all these functions.

No one need feel lonely at Tunbridge Wells.

"On the Walks you have all the liberty of conversation in the world, and any person that looks like a gentleman and has an agreeable address and behaves with decency and good manners, may single out whom he pleases that does not appear engaged, and may talk, rally, be merry and say any decent thing to them. But all this makes no acquaintance, nor is it understood to mean so. If a gentleman desires to be more intimate, he must do it by Proper Application, and not by ordinary meeting on the Walks."

Tunbridge Wells "is calculated to afford domestic accommodation to almost every class of visitor, from the Prince and Princess with appropriate retinue, to the solitary bachelor in sulky sinlessness". The approaches to the town were the haunts of "a parcel of mean fellows whom they called Touters, and their business touting. These men ride out miles to meet coaches and company coming hither and beg their custom while here". Sarah Porter was called the Queen of the Touters, and for some years before 1739 Beau Nash made use of her to collect subscriptions in the Rooms. She knew everyone's relations, and she boasted she never forgot a face. "She would stand in the ballroom and make thousands of curtesies and then she took her book, pen and ink, and followed people all over the room. No swearing or cursing disturbed her temper, and she said she was descended from those English women in the time of the Danes, who cut all their husbands' throats the first night of their marriage." Although Beau Nash thus made use of touting at Tunbridge Wells, the custom did not originate there. It is said to have begun on the Epsom Road on Derby Day, and got its name because the touters went "as far as Tooting in pursuit of the victims of their trade".

With the coming of railways, people travelled far more frequently and far more rapidly from place to place. The result was
that manners and customs in most countries became more
uniform. Etiquette books were less in demand and the amusing
guide books of the past were superseded by the universal Mr.
Bradshaw. There were still occasionally guide books on the old
lines, published by railway companies, and in a Folkestone Guide
of the 'fifties the following hopeful prophecy appears. It has alas !
not been fulfilled.

"Steam will prove a universal peacemaker. The natives of all
counties will cease to regard each other as enemies. Man will
meet Man as his brother. *War will cease.* Similar reflections to
these will naturally suggest themselves to the visitors while
lounging on the Pier."

2 Buried in the Past

IN THESE DAYS, WHEN SIGNPOSTS ALL OVER THE COUNTRY
have been temporarily mislaid, it is well to remember that
the goals of some of our most enjoyable pre-war expeditions
were not indicated in that conspicuous and now discredited
manner. The archæologist has never delighted in a building
which merely stands upon the common earth to be seen with
half an eye by the casual wayfarer. His treasure is hid in a field,
"which when he hath found it, he hideth, and for joy thereof,
goeth and selleth all that he hath and buyeth that field".

Archæologists are among the most combative of men, and as
I presume they exist in every country, I have often wished that
all quarrelsome statesmen could be forcibly made into excavators.
The fighting instinct would then have full scope. Swords would
be beaten into spades, and spears into pickaxes. The Bren gun
would give place to the sieve, and the tank to the wheelbarrow.
The Molotoff bread basket would drop the two first words of
its name, and would be occupied in carrying "finds". And best
of all this "war" would never end. There would always be a
new campaign to begin, and its battlefields would embrace the
whole world.

For even when two schools of archæologists reach the same conclusion, they differ so bitterly as to the routes by which they have arrived, that the war becomes more than ever acute. Take, for instance, the age of Stonehenge. In 1901 Sir Norman Lockyer decided that it was built between 1900 and 1500 B.C. He said that it was astronomically proved that only in that period did the sun rise so exactly behind the Hele Stone as to throw its shadow precisely upon the Altar Stone on the longest day. At present the actual sunrise on that day is a few degrees out. To the amateur this seemed a most satisfactory way of proving the point; and when excavations at the base of the stones revealed that the tools and objects buried under them pointed to 1800 B.C. as being the most likely date, it seemed that the watcher of the sky and the searcher in the earth had found a common meeting-place where, like righteousness and peace, they might kiss each other. Not at all. The date might be approximately correct, but the method of approach was appalling. Excavators pointed out that Stonehenge was built in days when there were no scientific means of astronomical observation. These calculations must have been done by the eye. And by shutting first one eye and then the other there was a possible variation in the date of about five hundred years.

Archæological field days mean extremely pleasant picnics. Motors arrive from all directions, and in the intervals of study the archæologists sit about in groups eating sandwiches and mayonnaise of salmon. But they are also as militant as most field days, for, of course, they are as controversial as any other archæological function. I well remember a clerical member of our society leading us for some miles over Salisbury Plain to see an earthwork which he had recently discovered, and which he considered to be the only instance in this country of an exact reproduction of a Greek theatre. It was a wonderful walk. The clergyman led the way, and about eighty people followed him. Round us was the boundless Plain; and as we proceeded I scanned the horizon, hoping to see come into view the vast and hitherto unrecognised outlines of an enormous amphitheatre. Our guide thought that his theatre must have been a meeting place for the wise men of three British villages which were known to have existed nearby. On we went. Vainly I tried to identify the vast discovery, and decided that my eye was not sufficiently trained. At last we arrived, and I had abruptly to bring my vision down from the telescopic to the microscopic. The theatre was tiny. It was like an armchair in a comfortable London club—a fairly high back, broad arms, and a low seat. In the great spaces around, it was not surprising that it had hitherto been overlooked.

The clergyman now expounded his views. He thought that when the three villages had business to discuss they had each sent a representative to this spot, and that the three sides of the tiny earthwork were the remains of their three seats. His lecture was accompanied by an undercurrent of interruption from a lady archæologist who disagreed with him.

"It's a dew pond", she said.

The old man lectured on undisturbed.

"It's a dew pond", came again.

He went on.

"It's a dew pond. It's a dew pond. It's a dew pond."

"No, madam. It has only three sides, so it never held water."

"It's a dew pond . . . a dew pond . . . Did you find any raddle and clay in the bottom?"

"No, madam, I did not. It is NOT A DEW POND."

The lecturer continued as though unaffected by this persistent heckler, but towards the end of his address he turned to her, saying ironically:

"You may be pleased to learn that a Henry II penny was found in the bank."

"I did not suggest that it was mediæval", she answered irately; and the whole party crowded on to the site to discuss their reaction to the controversy.

Another time, again on Salisbury Plain, we assembled to inspect a British village site, which had only lately been discovered. This was expected to be of supreme interest, as the site was on virgin down and had never been ploughed up.

I heard my neighbours saying: "We shall find it just as they left it. It will be most instructive".

This really did excite me. In my ignorant way, I at once imagined the dear little cave dwellings suddenly deserted, with all their furniture and belongings: kettles still on hobs, ornaments still on mantelpieces, beds still made.

7

Sustained by passionate enthusiasm I strode over the Plain in the wake of a goodly number of business-like archæologists. At one place they paused, and seemed to wait for stragglers to join for the last lap. I paused too, and looked across the uninterrupted spaces of green down.

"Wonderful! Wonderful!" I heard on all sides. I looked round the vast horizon and agreed. Then, to my dismay, I found that instead I must look under my feet. We were already at the village, and absolutely nothing of it could be recognised by the untrained eye. One by one we were shown the unique details of this remarkable prehistoric encampment. This hardly-visible depression in the turf was said to be a hearth. That one was a garden. Here had once been a boundary wall.

That this should disappoint, merely means that one is not an archæologist; yet nevertheless these expeditions were supremely enjoyable. Archæology then is more than a pursuit for experts. It is a real bit of the country, and appeals equally to the novice in historical study, to the lover of the countryside and to the simple person who merely enjoys the society of his fellow men.

My earliest recollections of archæologists are that they were all very old. They were retired admirals and archdeacons. But now anyone living in a part of the world where excavations are being carried on will take part, whatever his age. Aeroplanes first carried archæology away from the exclusive control of the elderly. Airmen are always young, and in the past twenty years or so, young men flying over wide stretches of country have taken photographs which have revolutionised the science of archæology. It was very exciting when aerial photographs first rediscovered the "Aubrey Holes" at Stonehenge, which for years had been derided as instances of the ridiculous credulity of that poetic seventeenth century scholar. Airmen found Wood-henge, a temple on the same lines as Stonehenge, situated a mile or two away, and originally built of wood. The impermanent material had perished; and the vast eternal stones nearby had obliterated all memory of the other building. Now its traces were seen from the air. Excavators discovered the situation of every post that had once stood in the temple, and they are now indicated by concrete blocks.

So archæology is a pursuit independent of milestones and signposts: its indicators are even more romantic. They also call for more imagination, and for an elasticity of mind which despises no method of approach. My most erudite friend, G. M. Young, is credibly said to have been the original of the Wise Scribe who brought out of his treasure things new and old. But though he can decipher any ancient manuscript in the British Museum, he also has the patient art of extracting what facts may lie behind the countryman's casual references to local conditions. Nowadays, when it is impossible to travel far afield, G. M. learns much from his comrades in the Home Guard, and where other people might see nothing but the uncritical credulity of the "uneducated", G. M. joins the fragments of living tradition on to his own previous store of authenticated information. This brings archæ-ology to life.

The discovery ten years ago of the "Sanctuary" near Avebury is an instance of progressive investigation. Nineteenth-century students doubted the existence of this monument, as they doubted the Aubrey Holes. Aubrey had mentioned it in about 1660; and Stukely made a sketch of it from memory soon after the winter of 1724, when the ground was ploughed "to gain a little dirty profit", and the Sanctuary was so completely destroyed that its very site seemed to be irrecoverable.

Fortunately, in the persons of Captain and Mrs. Cunnington, Wiltshire still possesses archæologists in the true line of succes-sion; and, after repeated efforts to identify the barrows and other landmarks mentioned in the old descriptions, they lighted upon a remark in Stukely's *Abury*. He is writing about the "fine group of barrows under Cherhill hill", at which point he thought that the Beckhampton Avenue ended. He goes on, "This point facing that group of barrows and looking up the hill, is a most solemn and awful place . . . and in this very point only, you can see the Temple on Overton Hill, on the south side of Silbury Hill".

These words gave the Cunningtons their long-sought indica-tion. Mrs. Cunnington writes, "On going to this spot, it was found that a small triangular patch of Mill Field, two-and-a-half miles away, could be seen; and by counting the telegraph poles visible along the roadside, it became easy to define the possible area on which the Sanctuary must have stood".

There it is, aeroplanes, telegraph poles and other modern "atrocities", the advent of which so greatly shocked our parents and grandparents, are now all brought into partnership with the indispensable spade in the discovery of the buried past.

The early archæologists were poets rather than scientists, but they were in many ways quite as reliable as their nineteenth-century successors. When Aubrey said that some of "the high stones of Stonehenge are honeycombed so deep that the starres doe make their nests in the holes", he is recording a truth as definite as any scientific fact. He sees it with a poet's eye, and this beauty of language, which belonged to the seventeenth century writers, sometimes made people inclined to discredit their facts. Really, Sir Richard Colt Hoare, who founded modern archæology in Wiltshire, was not so near the earth as his poetic predecessors; for while they wrote of what they themselves had seen, the charming and popular Sir Richard went forth on an excavating excursion, employed a gang of labourers, paid them well, and then left them to get on with the digging, while he lunched long and well with the Squire. When the meal was over Sir Richard returned to the scene of action, and was shown the specimens which the workmen had found. They had decided what was worth keeping, and Sir Richard never saw exactly how or where the discoveries had been made. In spite of this, his historical insight has never been excelled.

General Pitt-Rivers was the first archæologist I can remember. He often stayed with my parents, and to a child he appeared both far taller and far more beautiful than the ordinary race of men. I still think of him when I read in the book of Genesis, that "there were giants on the earth in those days". The records of his work can still be seen in his little museum at Farnham, where there exists a wonderful catalogue of the exhibits, every one of which is illustrated by the most careful, exact and delicate drawings in ink.

But although the giants of archæology have passed away as a race, perhaps the men of to-day are even more than giants. They are learning to pass on their studies from one generation to another, and so to vanquish their own mortality. We may criticise Sir Richard Colt Hoare for being limited to the science of his own day, but few people can see further than their own eyes will carry. Mr. Keiller, the learned and enthusiastic excavator of Avebury, has taught the world of archæologists how to pass the process of scientific discovery from one generation to another. When he began to excavate an extremely interesting and unusual camp on Windmill Hill, he decided that future generations might advance still further in their technique. Our investigations might possibly leave out just what they wanted to know. He therefore excavated half of the site; made copious and exact reports on it; covered it up again, and handed it over, with the undeveloped part, to the nation, on the understanding that no further investigation should take place for a hundred years. This is indeed selfless devotion to the cause of science.

There is near me a site which is of historical, though not archæological, interest, and during the years immediately preceding the war, some very exciting work was being done on it. It is Clarendon Palace. This famous building had disappeared as completely as "the Courts where Jamshỳd gloried and drank deep", although it had remained a favourite hunting place of the English kings until the time of Henry VII. It was now a legend. Farm buildings for ten miles round were made of stones and bricks quarried from its walls; and the village people said that a great chair of solid gold was somewhere buried in the ruins of the palace. There still remained a footpath which at all seasons of the year was miraculously green; and this was said to have been the one used by St. Thomas à Becket when he was "a cure priest at Winterbourn, and did use to go up to a chapell in Clarendon Parke to say masse". From the site of the lost palace could still be seen the glorious view over Salisbury and Old Sarum which delighted the Plantagenet courtiers and their ladies when they returned from the chase; but trees and ragged undergrowth covered the broad plateau upon which the palace itself had stood. The excavation of Clarendon shows how, nowadays, every kind of person delights to join in the search for lost historical monuments. Professor and Mrs. Tancred Borenius started the work, and carried out the chief part of it themselves, assisted by another expert in the person of Mr. John Charlton. The Christie Millers, who own the site, were among the keenest of the searchers. A party of University undergraduates spent weeks there in the summer vacation. Working men from the surrounding villages showed themselves natural archæologists, and unemployed miners from South Wales were of course masterly diggers. The result of all this work was that the ground-plan of the palace was slowly revealed. The walls of the great hall still remained standing up to a certain level, and this hall was approached by a broad stairway leading from the kitchen. The fourteenth century tiles were still in their places on the floor of the queen's apartments; and what most of all excited the experts was the discovery of the only mediæval tile-kiln not associated with a religious house. Here the Clarendon tiles had been made and baked; here they were laid in position; here they remained to be found in 1935.

Less than half of the palace has yet come back to light, but I hope that this work will be carried on when peace returns to the countryside.

3 Literary Pilgrimages

THERE ARE PARTS OF ENGLAND WHERE THE PILGRIM HAS no need of signposts. His way is illumined by a lighthouse which cannot be blacked-out even to-day, for it shines with "the light that never was on sea or land, the consecration and the Poet's dream". I mean those neighbourhoods which are associated with the names of poets and artists. To these we have always made pilgrimages, and to them we can still find our way.

If I think first of the Lake Country, perhaps it is because Wordsworth not only lived there, but wrote a *Guide to the Lakes*, and a guide, moreover, which was famous enough for Matthew Arnold to affirm that one of the earliest pilgrims to the Poet's Shrine asked Mr. Wordsworth whether he had ever written anything except the *Guide to the Lakes*. I know one ought to think that man a buffoon, but personally, I love him—his candour and his taste. Wordsworth is a guide well worth following to-day. And he remains so in spite of the fact that he violently attacked the railway as an approach to the Lakes, and I can guess what he would think of the motor-bus. He wrote that "the wide-spread waters . . . the steep mountains and the rocky glens" could only "be profitably enjoyed by a mind disposed to peace. . . . Go to a pantomime, a farce or a puppet-show", he says, "if you want noisy pleasure—the crowd of spectators who partake your enjoyment will, by their presence and acclamations, enhance it."

But it must not be thought that Wordsworth is out of touch with the spirit of to-day, for his suggested approach to the Lake Country was completely twentieth century. He invites the pilgrim to reach it by air. He tells his imaginary companion to "suppose our station to be upon a cloud hanging midway between the mountains of Great Gavel and Scawfell";—from there he will see the whole country spread out before him.

In other ways Wordsworth's Guide is still a useful book to take to the Lake Country. It is still apposite to remind the pilgrim that "Fastidiousness is a wretched travelling companion", and the poet makes no secret that he who is fastidious about the weather will miss much of the magic of the Lake Country. He admits that "it has been ascertained that twice as much rain falls here as in many parts of the island", but he glories in the beauty of "the showers, darkening, or brightening, as they fly from hill to hill", and in the "Vapours descending towards the valleys with inaudible motion" which "give a visionary character to everything around them". So it is that there often occur in the Lake Country "days which are worth whole months".

But Wordsworth is not always in the clouds, and he comes down to earth in his record of how this country of lake and mountain, of waterfall, stream and tarn, nevertheless owes much of its character and beauty to those who have lived there in past days. The Lords of the Manor, the Abbots, the shepherds, the dalesmen and the "statesmen" have left behind them the buildings in which they lived and worked, all fulfilling their own functions and imparting an individual beauty to the scene.

This brings us to Wordsworth's own Lakeland homes, none of which are described in his Guide, but all of which now attract the traveller. Cockermouth, where he was born, lies just outside the Lake Country, but when he came back to Westmorland as a man he lived in three different houses—"Dove Cottage" and "Allan Bank" at Grasmere, and "Rydal Mount" a few miles away. Dove Cottage is the place of pilgrimage, and nowhere else can there be a house which so completely holds the fragrance of those early days as does this little cottage, described day by day in Dorothy's diary, and with its garden still filled with flowers descended from those she planted. The brother and sister arrived at Dove Cottage at 4.30 in the darkening afternoon of December 20, 1799, and years afterwards old Molly Fisher, their next-door neighbour, told Dorothy she "mun never forget t'laal striped gown and t'laal straw bonnet as ye stood here". Every inch of the cottage and garden comes to life in Dorothy's journal, and indeed their diminutiveness is such that every inch tells. There never can have been so tiny a place which held so much. The orchard, still reached by the little stone steps which William built, must be the smallest orchard ever made—a narrow space of green in which it is possible to stand and touch the two sides by stretching out one's arms. A green linnet, or a butterfly, would be quite prominent inhabitants of this doll's orchard. And all about this homely paradise there spread "the Intimations of Immortality" for the Ode was written in the orchard. Thanks to Dorothy, it is possible to place and to date the writing of many of Wordsworth's most exquisite lyrical poems in the few feet covered by the house, the garden and the orchard.

Stratford-on-Avon is not so remote as the Lake Country, and in his native town Shakespeare is almost buried under Shakespeariana. In spite of this, one still feels with Edward Fitzgerald that to visit Stratford is "an event in one's life". One shares his impression. "It was not the town itself", he wrote, "or even the church that touched me most; but the old Footpaths over the Fields which He must have crossed three Centuries ago."

William Hall visited Stratford in 1694 and he says that the well-known inscription above Shakespeare's grave was written by the poet to suit "the capacity of clerks and sextons, for the most part a very ignorant set of people". Hall thinks that but for this curse the sexton would certainly have transferred Shakespeare's remains to the bone-house. These are the lines which checked that sexton's sacrilege:

> GOOD FREND FOR JESUS SAKE FORBEARE,
> TO DIGG THE DUST ENCLOASED HEARE:
> BLESTE BE YE MAN YT SPARES THES STONES,
> AND CURST BE HE YT MOVES MY BONES.

So though his admirers have not disturbed his coffin, they have made his native town into a sarcophagus.

Yet the little streets remain; and many of the houses; and

37   Lakeland Shepherd

38   Dinner-time on a North Country Farm

39   Summer in Shakespeare's Country

the river; and the meadows; and the way to Shottery where
Anne Hathaway lived. The plays themselves tell us some of the
memories which Shakespeare carried with him out of his boyhood, sometimes a little picture which is meaningless to anyone
who knows nothing of his childhood; sometimes a romantic
episode, embedded in his writing like a precious stone in a mine,
and giving unconscious testimony to "the hole of the pit whence"
it was "digged". Shakespeare's works contain many allusions
indicating memories of Stratford-on-Avon between the years
1575 and 1585.

Fortunately for us there has been in recent years a literary
pilgrim to Stratford-on-Avon who made some most revealing
discoveries. Madame Longworth de Chambrun stayed for some
time in the neighbourhood, and she pottered about among old
leases, records and the reports of coroners' inquests. In her
Shakespeare: Actor—Poet, she brings Shakespeare's Stratford to life,
by reviving all kinds and sorts of people who lived about it in
his day, people whom he may, or may not, have known personally, but whose figures filled the streets he walked in. They
were the subjects of conversation and gossip in the days when the
young poet was gathering his impressions.

All visitors to Stratford know Shakespeare's birthplace, but
all may not know that his father did not occupy the whole house.
Madame de Chambrun's researches into contemporary Warwick-
shire leases discovered that the house was then divided into
three. The Shakespeares lived in the middle one of these, having
as neighbours on either side Richard Horneby, the blacksmith,
and William Wedgwood, the tailor. This throws new light upon
Hubert's description in *King John* of the crowd brought into the
street by the rumour that the French had landed:

> I saw a smith stand with his hammer, thus,
> The whilst his iron did on the anvil cool,
> With open mouth swallowing a tailor's news;
> Who with his shears and measure in his hand
> Standing on slippers (which his nimble haste
> Had falsely thrust upon contrary feet)
> Told of a many thousand warlike French.

To recall to life that one scene alone makes it worth while to
go to Stratford and to stand where that little boy stood nearly
four hundred years ago.

8

In the accounts of coroners' inquests, Madame de Chambrun found some most telling evidence. In the very year of Shakespeare's birth, a macabre tragedy took place in the town, and as it concerned the family of one of the principal townsmen, no doubt it was talked of for years in the hearing of the little boy.

A young woman named Charlotte Clopton was buried in her family vault, which was re-opened some years later for another burial. Then it was found that Charlotte must have been in a trance when they thought her dead. She had awoken and got off her bier, to dash her head vainly against the door of the tomb, and in her unavailing struggles to break her way to daylight, she had seized as tools the dead men's bones that lay about on the ground. She was still clutching them in her hands when they found her.

This frightful story must have haunted Shakespeare, and he makes Juliet say, before she drinks the fatal draught:

> O! if I wake, shall I not be distraught,
> Environed with all these hideous fears,
> And madly play with my forefather's joints?
> And pluck the mangled Tybalt from his shroud?
> And, in this rage, with some great kinsman's bone,
> As with a club, dash out my desperate brains.

Madame de Chambrun came upon the report of another coroner's inquest which took place in Stratford when Shakespeare was sixteen. Here one reads the story of Katherine Hamlett's death. The girl was found drowned, after an unhappy love affair, and the jury had to decide whether or no they should return a verdict of *felo de se*. The parents pleaded that the girl had died by accident, for at the place where the body was found, a great willow leant across the stream, and her clothes were entangled in its roots. It was contended that she had climbed upon the tree trunk and bent over to dip in the stream the flowers which were found in her hand. There is no doubt that the Queen in *Hamlet* knew this tragic story, for she says:

> There is a willow grows ascaunt the brook,
> That shews his hoar leaves in the glassy stream;
> Therewith fantastic garlands did she make
> Of crow-flowers, nettles, daisies, and long purples. . . .
> There on the pendent boughs her coronet weeds
> Clambering to hang, an envious sliver broke;
> When down her weedy trophies, and herself,
> Fell in the weeping brook.

The evidence given by the witnesses at this inquest is largely reproduced in the talk of Shakespeare's gravediggers.

A pilgrimage to Woodbridge and its neighbourhood is to step into that world of Edward Fitzgerald's, where there is neither earth nor sea, but only atmosphere. He seems to have been one with the quiet, anonymous sweep of sea and land which blend together to make East Anglia. The very names of his correspondents—Cowell, Lowell and the like—have captured the rounded echoes of those amphibious distances, and to spend a few days in Fitzgerald's country is like peacefully sitting with Sabrina Fair,

"Under the glassy, cool, translucent wave."

Edward Fitzgerald's translation of Omar Khayyám was one of the famous books of the nineteenth century, but in it you may look in vain for the translator. Nor can you catch this elusive being in the Calderon Plays. He wished to be unrecognised, and that is why he gave his great poetic gifts chiefly to the task of translating other men's masterpieces. But you do get him in his letters, and in them he lives to-day.

Yet he remains elusive, for we, who only read the letters, in many ways know as much of him as his correspondents did. He summed himself up when he wrote to John Allen:

"My paper is done, talking about these dead and gone, whom you and I have only known in print; and yet as well so, as most we know in person. I really find my Society in such Books."

That this is true is shown by a remark in a letter of 1876 addressed to Mrs. Kemble. He writes of Tennyson, one of his regular correspondents, and apparently one of his closest friends:

"And now—Who should send in his card to me last week but the old poet himself. 'Dear old Fitz', ran the card in pencil, 'We are passing thro'.' I had not seen him for twenty years."

So even his contemporaries seem to have existed for him most really on paper, and we are probably as close to "old Fitz" as they were. He is to us what Madame de Sevigné, Dickens and Walter Scott were to him. He belongs to what de Vogue calls "La Société idèale que tout pays se compose avec sa literature classique".

We can, then, think of Fitzgerald as actually living, as he said, "a lonely life"; and although I am told that he had a wife for a short time, I have never been able to find the letter in which he mentions her. I shall therefore continue to look upon him as the old bachelor that he always seemed to be.

This timeless existence finds its perfect setting in Suffolk. Even when Fitzgerald writes (as he rarely does) of actual living people, they assume a dreamlike, remote character, passing like figures seen in a glass. He himself remarks on this when he is staying in his father's house at Wherstead.

"All our family, except my mother, are collected here: all my brothers and sisters, with their wives, husbands and children sitting at different occupations, or wandering about the grounds and gardens, discoursing each their separate concerns, but all united into one whole. When I see them passing to and fro, and hear their voices, it is like the scenes in a play."

There was a time in his life when Fitzgerald was constantly acquiring, renting or buying fresh houses in the Woodbridge neighbourhood; but he seldom lived in these houses when once he possessed them. Instead, he handed them over to his nine nieces, while he himself roamed the sea in his yacht, or lived in lodgings at Aldeburgh or Lowestoft. So it is in the air round Woodbridge, rather than in any particular house, that the pilgrim meets the spirit of old Fitz. Here he seems eternally to remain in the "green idleness" which so delighted him in his lifetime. "Everything is fun in the country", was a proverb which he quoted (or probably invented), and he says that he revelled in the "dullness of country people", which he infinitely preferred to "the impudence of Londoners". He scoffed at the conducted lecture tours round the Mediterranean coasts that were only then beginning, and said that "Suffolk turnips seem to me so classical compared to all that sort of thing".

When Fitzgerald writes of his Woodbridge world, his mind ranges far beyond the boundaries of his own estate. When he walked in the Seckhouse Almshouse garden "till 9 p.m. in a sharp frost", he did not flatten his nose against the almsmen's windows to watch their little doings inside: what he saw was "Orion stalking over the south before me". When he "looked out at about ten o'clock at night before going to bed, it seemed perfectly still; frosty, and the stars shining bright. I heard a continuous moaning sound, which I knew to be, not that of an infant exposed, or female ravished, but of the sea more than ten miles off". Dunwich is, perhaps, the place which speaks most

40, 41   Suffolk Pastorals

42   George Herbert's Bemerton, *ca.* 1840

43 The Wiltshire Downs

of all of the man himself, and of the peculiar character of the country he loved and still haunts. Here, he says, "are the Village remains of a once large Town devoured by the sea: and, yet undevoured (except by Henry VIII), the grey walls of a Grey Friars' Priory, beside which they used to walk, under such sunsets as illumine them still. . . . Robin Redbreast was piping in the Ivy along the Walls; and, under them, Blackberries ripening from stems which those old Grey Friars picked from".

Fitzgerald could humanise those wide empty spaces. He is never swallowed up by them, but comes into his own in this desolate, timeless world—a friendly spirit, who might be met any evening walking there on the wet sands, lovable, and very near at hand. And then, he would not be there at all.

Fitzgerald made many a literary pilgrimage, and quite early in his life, he went "to Salisbury to see the Cathedral, but more to walk to Bemerton, George Herbert's village. It is about a mile and a half from Salisbury alongside a pleasant stream with old-fashioned water-mills beside: through fields very fertile. When I got to Bemerton, I scarcely knew what to do with myself. It is a very pretty Village with the Church and Parsonage much as Herbert must have left it. . . . The people in the cottages had heard of a pious man named Herbert, and had read his books—but they don't know where he lies. . . . I thought I must have passed the spot in the road where he assisted the man with the fallen horse: and, to show the benefit of good examples, I was serviceable that very evening in the Town to some people coming in a cart: for the driver was drunk, and driving furiously home from the races, and I believe would have fallen out, but that some folks, of whom I was one, stopped the cart".

Since 1832, when this was written, the quiet meadows through which Herbert walked to hear evensong in the cathedral have been flanked by some particularly incongruous factory buildings, and by an engine-house attached to Salisbury station. Yet it is possible to turn one's back upon these reminders of a century which preferred mechanics to meditation, and to find many a point from which one can see Herbert's water meadows and his view of the cathedral exactly as they were in the seventeenth century. Perhaps the village people do not read his books so much as their great-grandfathers did, but they know his name; for did they not all take part, a few years back, in a pageant to

9

commemorate the 300th anniversary of his death? Fitzgerald found no memorial at Bemerton to this village saint, and thought of asking permission to erect one himself; but since then, a fine parish church in the nineteenth century "Early English" style has been built in his memory, and in the tiny church which faces the parsonage there is now a good modern window which commemorates him. The medlar he planted grows on in the rectory garden, where the trout stream ripples towards Salisbury. The George Herbert pilgrim should not only visit Bemerton and Fugglestone to see the churches in which Herbert ministered: he should also stroll in the meadows to the south of the village, where the herons fly overhead, and the men call their cows home in the primitive language that George Herbert knew.

Some years ago, an ardent American lady was travelling by train through Dorset. Her one fellow-passenger was an old gentleman of distinguished appearance and obviously of an autocratic disposition. The ardent lady gazed on the landscape which flashed past the firmly shut windows of the compartment. It hastened by, and she saw landmark after landmark pass out of sight. She could bear it no longer. She addressed her companion, regardless of his absorption in *The Times*.

"Forgive me, sir", she said. "This is the Hardy country, is it not?"

He dropped his newspaper.

"The Hardy country?" he ejaculated, in the tone of a startled thunderclap. "No, indeed. It's MY country. I have hunted it for the last thirty years."

His voice tailed off into a cantankerous murmur:

"Hardy, indeed! Who is the fellow?"

But it *was* the Hardy country, and there is no stretch of land in England which a writer has made so completely his own. He gave back to it the long-forgotten historic name which now trips off the tongues of library subscribers who never heard of the Heptarchy, and who probably imagine that Wessex is a "portmanteau" word coined by Mr. Hardy to give the sound of some of the counties in which he set his books.

It was an achievement, this re-creating of the old Kingdom of Wessex, "putting it back on the map", as they say, and this not only for scholars (who presumably had heard of it before), but

44   "A Few Crusted Characters"

45 "A Very Temple of the Winds"

for the man-in-the-street. A literary pilgrimage to the Hardy country is memorable for more than one reason. Here Thomas Hardy was born, lived the greater part of his life, and here he died. He belonged to it. Then, all his writing is framed in it— his novels, his poems, and even his great European drama of " The Dynasts " keeps homing to the birthplace of its creator. And if Hardy had never lived, the county of Dorset would still possess a loveliness to steal the heart away. It is the perfect county to walk in, with its empty downlands, where the sea breaks in upon the landscape like a great "Amen" closing a vast chorus. It has its Roman roads, and its prehistoric ridgeways, following the contour of the hills, and leading the mind back to those primitive days when human settlements were determined by the lie of the land. There is a particularly lovely green road which runs from the Isle of Purbeck almost to Abbotsbury, with the sea a few miles distant during the whole of its length. That road is of the essence of Dorset.

The part of Wessex which lies in Dorset is the district most connected with Hardy, but a map of the country covered by his books includes the whole of the old Kingdom, from Wantage to the Dorset coast, and from the Devon border to the New Forest. His whole being was impregnated with the world of Wessex—its bare downs, which curve like a horizon at sea; its village churches, with their unpretentious towers lifted towards the distant sky; its men and women who follow the old trades— farmers, millers, blacksmiths, soldiers and sailors. This country and these people are all *within* Hardy, and he in them. They are the substance of his bones and of his mind. They are the ink in which he dips his pen. There is for Hardy no such thing as "local colour". Dorset has given its infinite tinge to his spirit.

There is a stage direction in that scene in "The Dynasts" which depicts the lighting of the beacon on Egdon Heath at the time of Napoleon's expected invasion:

"Something in the feel of the darkness and in the personality of the spot imparts a sense of uninterrupted space around, the view by day extending from the cliffs of the Isle of Wight eastward, to Blackdon Hill by Deadman's Bay westward, and south across the valley of the Froom to the ridge that screens the Channel."

No dark night could blot out for Hardy the "personality" of any spot in his own county. He knew the "feel" of it.

One final passage will show that Hardy was the supreme guide to one of the most famous sites in Wessex. Here he gives the sense of Wessex by night in a very poignant setting. The chapter is one of the last ones in *Tess of the d'Urbervilles*, when, after the murder of Alex, Angel and Tess are escaping by night from the police.

"All around was open loneliness and black solitude, over which a stiff breeze blew.

"They had proceeded thus gropingly two or three miles further when on a sudden Clare became conscious of some vast erection close in his front, rising sheer from the grass. They had almost struck themselves against it.

" 'What monstrous place is this'? said Angel.

" 'It hums', said she. 'Hearken!'

"He listened. The wind, playing upon the edifice, produced a booming tune, like the note of some gigantic one-stringed harp. No other sound came from it, and lifting his hand and advancing a step or two, Clare felt the vertical surface of the wall. It seemed to be of solid stone, without joint or moulding. Carrying his fingers onward he found that what he had come in contact with was a colossal rectangular pillar; by stretching out his left hand he could feel a similar one adjoining. At an indefinite height overhead something made the black sky blacker, which had the semblance of a vast architrave uniting the pillars horizontally. They carefully entered beneath and between; the surfaces echoed their soft rustle; but they seemed to be still out of doors. The place was roofless. Tess drew her breath fearfully, and Angel perplexed, said:

" 'What can it be?'

"Feeling sideways they encountered another tower-like pillar, square and uncompromising as the first; beyond it another and another. The place was all doors and pillars, some connected above by continuous architraves.

" 'A very Temple of the Winds', he said. . . . 'It is Stonehenge'."

THE FOURTH MOOD

SUBJUNCTIVE

46, 47   Summer Silhouettes

48   Fun of the Fair

1 Buying and Selling

MEAN TO CONSIDER THE SUBJUNCTIVE AS THE MOOD OF PER-
sonal contacts, and, from very primitive days, barter seems to
have been the first of these; while buying and selling have
always been looked upon as an excuse for pleasure. Fairs and
markets were for centuries the chief social functions, and
though fairs have lost their position as practically the only
occasions for general conviviality, market days have not yet been
superseded by anything else. A market town is still a provincial
metropolis. In every county it is there that local life is focused,
and the whole countryside converges once a week upon its
market town. The County Magistrates generally sit near the
market place, so that men can freely pass from one kind of
business to the other. Wives accompany their husbands to
"town" for a good day's shopping—not, as formerly, in the
phæton, the gig or the tax-cart, but now in the motor-car.
And working people from the villages, who used to fill the
carriers' carts, now ride by motor-bus. At about four o'clock
in the afternoon of market day, one of the chief sights of a market
town is the setting forth of those great fleets of buses. For an
hour or so beforehand, the passengers have been assembling,
laden with baskets and parcels and "shopping bags", bubbling
with gossip and local jokes, and distracted by the loss of a child
or two, or by the non-appearance of an expected parcel. At
last everyone is aboard, and the great vehicle swings slowly out
of its harbour, to feel its way through the traffic, which is
organized by rule-of-thumb rather than by any of the better
known traffic laws.

There was a memorable scene in Salisbury one market day,
a year or two ago, when a new bus station was to be opened. The
ceremony began with a luncheon in the Council House, and then
the Mayor of Salisbury, and I, as Mayor of Wilton, proceeded
formally to declare the station open. We crossed the market
place at the head of a small procession, which grew rapidly as

67

the assembled people caught sight of our dignity and our chains, and eventually arrived on the scene at the head of a considerable crowd. Our first business was to cut two coloured ribbons which had been stretched across the entrance to the station, and then there immediately appeared the first bus which was to use it. In order to prevent delay, this had filled up at its old starting-point, and it was already crowded with passengers for Andover. They had no idea they were going to take part in any function. There they sat in their places, hugging their parcels, and staring out of the windows with astonishment at what must have looked to them like an unruly crowd of rioters waiting to spring upon them. Perhaps they were reassured by finding that this mob was headed by two Mayors in their robes, each holding aloft a pair of grape scissors. But their fears returned when these Mayors addressed them with loud and passionate prayers:

"God bless this bus. May you have a safe journey. May this bus pass safely through all the dangers of the road", and other slogans equally suggesting that this particular journey to Andover was likely to be a ticklish one.

It was a typical market day festivity, for in a market town the chief dates are always made for market days, because then the buses arrive from everywhere, and the village people swell the population of the town. If you want to be certain of running up against any or all of your country neighbours, you are sure to meet them in the market place on market day.

But these assignations and festivities are merely sideshows, distinct from the main business and interest of the day. People have come for buying and selling, and that is what they mean to do. All through the morning the sales of cattle and sheep, pigs and poultry, are in full swing. The auctioneers stand in their rostrums, roaring out their racy descriptions of the various lots. They all possess considerable knowledge of the points of live-stock, and plenty of native wit to season this knowledge. The leading auctioneers have each a special standing in the world of agriculture. The value of their opinions has been tested by time, and their sales depend upon it. A good auctioneer is admitted to be an expert, and as such he compels attention. The reputation that he has built up determines the amount of his business, and also the prices he can command. Then it is essential that he should possess what sailors call "a gale o' wind voice"; for it has got to prevail over a tempest of male conversation, which is loudly carried on all round him, and is interspersed with roars of laughter, sometimes at the jokes he has made himself, but equally often at private jokes circulating among his clientèle.

These sales go on throughout the morning, and they are followed by what used to be called the "Farmers' Ordinary", which means the mid-day dinner in the chief hotels of the town. English cooking is often decried, but these masculine meals show it at its unbeatable best. Farmers know a good joint of meat when they see one, and they also know how it should be cooked and sent up. They demand, and they get, the best meat obtainable in the countryside; while, even for a mere woman, who is not admitted to the meal, there are few more exhilarating sounds than the roars of talk and laughter which burst out of the dining room whenever the door is opened, and which eventually surge to a climax when the party breaks up.

As well as the important sales of stock, a good deal of other lively buying and selling takes place on market day. The market place is crowded with stalls, on which are displayed the smaller country products—fruit, vegetables, eggs, and (especially on stalls stocked by Women's Institutes) jams and pickles, honey and cakes. There are glass and china stalls, upon which has been thrown a jumble of unrelated cups and saucers, jugs and plates. Old books can also be bought in markets; and many an old bookworm can be seen pawing and poring over a motley collection of tattered magazines, well-thumbed volumes of sermons and dirty school books, in the hope of discovering among them a choice and hitherto unidentified First Edition. A slowly moving crowd circulates with gloating eyes and disdainful tongues round and round the stalls. Prices are vigorously contested. The stallkeepers avow that theirs are the cheapest goods in the market. Housewives scoff at them, and loudly tell each other where better and even cheaper things of the same kind can be found over the way. Groups of people from far-off villages meet with animated gestures of surprise and with loud delight, and then they block the way for a quarter-of-an-hour while they all in turn relate the history of their lives since they last met. No one complains of this holding up of the traffic. All the marketers are there for the day, and most of the pleasure of their visit to town lies in these unforeseen, but always

10

anticipated, encounters with old friends. The largest crowd collects round the cheapjack, who not only produces watches from his pocket with the ease of a conjuror, but makes the welkin ring with startling and realistic descriptions of diseases and their cures. An extraordinary old fellow was for years a familiar sight in our town. He wore a ginger-coloured dressing gown and dark spectacles; and a short stiff grey beard added importance to his countenance. Holding up a bottle filled with a deep purple, murky, thick and mottled liquid, he roared out:

"That's the inside o' your stomach."

After a dramatic pause, while he held the exhibit on high, he continued:

"Now, see what one of my pills will do for it."

Out came a bottle of pills, and one was thrown into the disgusting concoction. As it floated down, the liquid became clear as the purest spring water. All the cloudiness vanished. It was a triumph of conjuring, and always brought a crowd of dyspeptic sufferers to exchange their shillings for a box of miraculous pills.

Although the real market dinners are the prerogative of the farmers, many other appetising meals are eaten on a market day. The tea-shops and milk-bars do a good trade from 11 o'clock onwards, when they invite their clients to enjoy their morning coffee. The tables are soon crowded, and as the day goes on, the doors keep opening to admit stout women, strung, each hour, with more and more parcels, who scan the scene with anxious eyes. There seems no possible space for themselves and their belongings. Then the anxiety changes to a sudden gleam of pleasure as a friend is espied, who signals that she will "move up" with a hospitable re-arrangement of plates and dishes, bundles and baskets, and thus allow the newcomer to "squeeze in". Those who imagine that there is little social life in the country would change their opinions if they spent a whole market day in a provincial town.

Cathedral cities and market towns came into being during the first of England's chief town building periods. The City Fathers of the thirteenth, fourteenth and fifteenth centuries gave beauty and character to their towns because they always saw them as entities standing in a certain relation to the country around. The cathedral, which contained the bishop's throne, would always be, in the mind of its founders, the religious centre of

49   Market Day a Hundred Years Ago

50   Salisbury Market To-day

51 Siesta

52 Wooden Horses

the surrounding diocese; and the city was planned to suit the convenience of ecclesiastics. The merchants saw a similar advantage in creating market towns for their districts, and there was great competition to secure market charters. This competition brought the mediæval inhabitants of Wilton and Salisbury literally to blows. The Salisbury merchants secured a market charter for their town, which had already become the ecclesiastical centre of the county through the new cathedral which was being built. The Wilton man foresaw the decay of their own long-established market, and they went out into the roads where they "waylaid and hindered, beat and stopped" the merchants on their way to Salisbury. These fisticuffs were of no avail, and Salisbury market won the day.

Fairs are a kind of holiday market.

Their *raison d'être* is business—the sale of sheep, cattle, horses or cheeses, and sometimes the hiring of farm servants; but, even more than markets, they have also always been opportunities for fun and merriment. Most people only attend them for the "fun of the fair", and the noises of a fairground are very festive. First of all, and most pervading, there is always to be heard the unending strains of the merry-go-round's harsh barrel-organ; but this is the background to other equally characteristic sounds. The pop of rifle shots as sportsmen fire at eggs which move miraculously up and down on jets of water. The bang and the bell of the strength-testing machine. The raucous invitation to *"come and see the fat woman"* or some other monstrosity. To these are sometimes added the roars of lions and tigers and the yelps of jackals, if a travelling menagerie is taking advantage of the fair to attract spectators. And then there is always the undercurrent of human voices, speaking in the dialect of the countryside, and so containing more tone and quality than can be heard in towns. Country vowel-sounds are richer and more numerous than town vowels. Consonants are stronger. Speech gains in variety and raciness.

Stalls at fairs display an extraordinary collection of completely worthless, really ugly and exceedingly cheap little trifles; and yet these "fairings" possess an inexplicable charm. They *are* "fairings"; and that is why everyone is impelled to carry home a crudely-printed handkerchief, a hideous china shepherdess or greyhound, a box with shells all over its lid, a sugar stick, and

10*

a bag of that thin, sticky, perforated gingerbread which only appears at fairs. That these things are bought, and bought by everybody, proves that the fair spirit is far more intoxicating than any party spirit in the world. When one is at the fair all these things become as seductive and desirable as a gross of spectacles seemed to be to Moses in *The Vicar of Wakefield*.

In spite of the country genius for making festivals out of buying and selling, nothing can prevent a Sale of Work from being a terribly dreary affair; yet every village must have at least one every summer. For weeks beforehand the whole parish is busy with preparations. A garden is lent; the morning arrives; the stalls are prettily arranged; and then, a few hours before the time fixed for the opening ceremony, the goods have to be hurriedly scrambled into the schoolroom to escape a deluge of rain. Everyone agrees to make the best of it. A leading lady of the neighbourhood declares the sale open. The clergyman makes a tactful speech. The members of the audience look feverishly round. There is nothing at all to buy, and no one at all to buy it. Yet the goods in view have a far better value than the "fairings" described above; but the sale of work has never succeeded in evoking that rollicking recklessness which takes possession of everyone who enters a fairground.

And yet, when all is over, the takings nearly always "beat last year's record"; and the sale is pronounced a business success.

On the other hand, a jumble sale is a wildly popular function. Scouts and guides traverse the village beforehand, collecting from every house of any size anything which is completely past using by its owner. On to the tables is piled a horrible conglomeration of old clothes, hats, boots, threadbare bits of carpet, pots and pans, kettles without bottoms, cracked plates and cups, burst travelling-bags, broken-down wheelbarrows, and whatnot. Directly the doors are open the mob bursts in. No need of any formal opening ceremony: the buyers could not wait for that. In they rush with their shopping bags, to fight over the best things, to turn them over, tumble and handle, to slip them surreptitiously into their bags if they can, and, if not, to pay the ridiculous price which is asked. To the looker-on the whole thing seems to be a nightmare, but to the buyers it is a ravishing dream. Like a sale of work, a jumble sale is a very paying thing.

2 Public Work

ONE REASON WHY PEOPLE IN THE COUNTRY ARE SO BUSY is that all classes take their share in public work. This greatly adds to the interest of country life. Of course there is even more public work to be done in towns; but then there are so many more people to do it that the community as a whole doesn't feel it at all. Important as is the work of the London County Council, for instance, most of the millions who live in the metropolis have no idea what it is doing. Whereas in the country nearly everybody plays a part.

County Councils and their committees give a great deal of hard work to those country gentlemen and large farmers who are public-spirited enough to abandon their daily avocations altogether for several days in each month. District Councils occupy men and women who cannot get so far afield. The Parish Councils are largely composed of working men and women, and so they meet in the evenings, after work is over. Then there are the Magistrates' Benches, and the Public Assistance Committees which have taken the place of the old Boards of Guardians. There are Diocesan Conferences, Ruri-decanal Meetings, Parochial Church Councils, and Free Church Councils. Each political party has its own organisation in every constituency. In most villages the men are busy with their committees of the British Legion, the Foresters, the Oddfellows and other clubs; and the women bustle to and from the Women's Institutes. Even the children are given a sense of responsibility as Scouts and Guides.

The country population is small, so all this means that most people have to pull their weight in one thing or another. These organisations bring people together, and greatly add to the interest of living in the country.

The Motoring Acts have much increased the labours of magistrates all over the country, but they have proportionately decreased the interest of their work. It has been calculated that 60 per cent. of the cases which come before magistrates nowadays are traffic cases; and throughout the country, indictable offences are only 10 per cent. of the whole. In 1888, 164 cases came before the County Bench on which I now sit: in 1940 there were close on 2,500. Yet crime has immensely decreased; and far the greater part of these cases dealt with motor lights, speed limits, "halt" signs or lack of driving licences. These cases are often extremely dull, but in spite of that we do see some curious little bits of human life. We see one isolated section of a personality. People appear before us, answer a few searching questions, listen to our sentence, pay their fines and go away. Vignettes of village life are set before us. A curious feature of a police court is that one's acquaintance with those who appear in it is so close and yet so transitory.

Surprising contrasts show themselves. Two motor vehicles collided at a cross-roads. One contained a professor of psychology who was driving two octogenarian ladies (his mother and his aunt) along a main road, when from a side road a motor coach ran into him. It contained eighteen fried-fish men proceeding from Blackpool to Bournemouth. The result of this disastrous collision was that one of the octogenarians was killed. Little did she think that morning, when she left home in the quiet company of a psychological professor, that, before night fell, eighteen fried-fish men would be responsible for her sudden death.

Another remarkable case occurred when a very poor looking woman appeared before us, charged with stealing a piece of tarpaulin, the property of a neighbouring farmer. The defendant was very out-at-elbows, and looked as if she had not got sixpence in the world. Her son, apparently about nineteen years of age, was charged with her. He looked weak in mind and body. We learnt that the woman had not attempted to conceal what she had done; and that, some months after the theft, the police discovered the tarpaulin, its owner's name still clearly painted upon it, placed over her aeroplane in one of her fields. We could hardly believe our ears on hearing that this dilapidated-looking woman was the owner of an aeroplane; and our astonishment was increased when we heard that she possessed not one but two.

"The second one is not a very good one, your Worships", said the sergeant who was giving evidence. "It was made by her son."

The defendant went into the witness-box, and said she was very sorry she had given way to this sudden and irresistible temptation which had overcome her as she caught sight of the tarpaulin when she drove past in her motor car.

"The defendant has a car, then?"

"Oh, yes, your Worships. The defendant has two cars. One is a Rolls-Royce."

This allegation roused the defendant to wrath.

"I wasn't driving my Rolls that morning. I never do drive it now. I only keep it for sentimental reasons, because it once belonged to Mr. William Whiteley, of Westbourne Grove."

That was the end. The poverty-stricken owner of two aeroplanes and two motor cars paid her fine and left the court, and we heard no more of her previous history. Nor did we know what happened to her afterwards. She was a ship that passed in the night.

A romantic and picturesque piece of Sherlock Holmes work was carried out one day by our local police inspector. We had before us a woman on a charge of dangerous driving. She had swung off the road at a bend, and ran for some distance along the grass verge till she collided with a telegraph post and came to grief. The police arrived, examined the damage, measured the road, and took all the other ordinary particulars. This occupied some time, after which the constable walked back a a few yards and saw a hole in the hedge which seemed to have been caused by the motor as it careered along on the green verge. He looked through this hole, and saw, in the cottage garden behind the hedge, an old woman lying dead. She had been knocked down by the motor and sent flying through the hedge, and the driver had declared that she had been quite unaware that there was anybody in her way. The police case was that this car had been driven recklessly for some miles, and two witnesses asserted that they saw this same car leave the road at a previous bend, where it ran along a high bank at an acute angle and seemed to be on the brink of overturning. The driver said this was not her car. It was quite untrue to say that she had left the road before. Then the police called a witness from fairyland. They handed us half of a green leaf which had grown on a poplar called by the exquisite name of the Wayfarer's tree. This leaf had evidently been torn from its stem by the car at some point very near the place of the accident, for it was found unfaded between the wing and the bonnet when the car crashed. The constable who found it showed it to his superior officer, and the two men searched the hedgerow for a specimen of the Wayfarer's tree. There was none to be found. But two miles back, at the point where wheel-marks indicated that the car had left the road and run along the bank, there stood the tree in question, and on it a broken twig. The torn green leaf was set before us, with beside it other leaves taken from the same tree. The little voiceless witnesses could not be gainsaid. They proved that the car had twice left the road.

The meetings of local committees of the Public Assistance Board are very long and very depressing, as these committees have no power at all, and are merely advisory. At the last Poor Law revision the old title of "Guardian to the Poor" was abolished. The Guardians became members of committees, and the Workhouses became "Institutions". These changes in nomenclature are supposed to be more considerate of the feelings of the applicants for relief: I know not why. In old days, all "indoor" cases were housed in workhouses as near as possible to their own homes; whereas now the different classes of cases are segregated and each Institution only deals with one class. This is doubtless more efficient than the old method, but it seems less humane, for sometimes the people have to be sent a long way from their homes, so that their friends can very seldom visit them.

Although the purpose of all the recent changes of nomenclature was to take away the sting from poor relief by setting it free from painful old associations, yet the new committees retain a dreary, Dickensian character. There had been a complaint about the bread supplied in an Institution which was under our care, and I cannot forget some words in the report which we asked for on the subject. "The bread is up to the standard for an Institution." This was after a dead mouse had been found in one of the loaves.

An even more macabre thing happened at another meeting, though this had its funny side. The business before us was selecting an undertaker for the coming year. The official rule is that, except in special cases, public authorities should take the lowest tender, and we opened the tenders from several firms. It was difficult to decide which was the lowest, for the charges for funerals were divided into several groups. "Still-borns." "Children under five." "Adults." The tenderer who charged least for "still-borns" charged most for "adults"; and for some time the members of the committee, armed with pencils and paper, tried to work out the average numbers of deaths at the different ages, in order to discover the lowest rate for the whole.

While this was being discussed, the Master of the Institution stood by, with an ironic smile on his face; and after we had been at it for some time, he interposed with:

"I don't expect we shall have many 'still-borns' this year. The maternity ward is closed. It is taken over by the military."

We agreed to cut out the "still-borns" altogether.

It may be said that in a book about the country there can surely be no mention of an office so urban as that of a Mayor; but I can't leave out the Mayor of Wilton, for of all the public work that I have done, nothing has meant so much to me as being the first woman mayor of my native town. Most boroughs are large and important. They are areas which are "built-up" or even overbuilt, where "life" cannot be called "country life". Yet, scattered about the country, there are a few very small, and also very ancient, towns whose pride it is to possess Mayors and Corporations. Of these the oldest is Wilton in Wiltshire.

I believe there is nothing in this country to-day more fundamentally "English" than these rural mayors, with their offices, their powers, their duties and their customs. They continue to function in the same manner and in the same happy and intimate relation to their boroughs, as did all mayors in the old days, before large cities, in the modern sense of the word "large", had begun to exist.

In the seventeenth century, the Mayor of Wilton was fined if he appeared outside his door without his red official robe, but nowadays this is kept for ceremonial occasions. It is a glorious pure red colour, very brilliant, and hanging in heavy folds which throw deep shadows. The mayor's chain, of silver gilt, is immensely heavy, and from it hangs a jewel, upon which is emblazoned in blue enamel and gold the ancient seal of the mayor. It is doubtful what this seal represents. At the Herald's Visitation of Wilts in 1623 it was described as "two Saxon Kings *sejant* in Gothic niches, crowned, with sceptres in their hands". Alternatively it has been interpreted as the "Coronation of the Virgin"; but whatever its subject it is a beautiful jewel. Wilton also possesses some very fine silver-gilt maces, one of which is a very delicate piece of work of the time of Charles I, and another an enormous and elaborate specimen of the goldsmith's art of the period of Charles II. The mayor's personal mace is a small, silver, Queen Anne one, which I suspect was also used to carry disinfectant herbs in time of plague, as there is a hidden hollow in its head. On state occasions, the mayor is accompanied in procession by four aldermen and twelve councillors, while a beadle carrying a tipstaff brings up the rear.

The Borough of Wilton is almost exactly a mile square, and it lies in a hollow in the downs at a place where two rivers meet. These two streams have become many, for the early inhabitants of Wilton used them to turn their mills in all parts of the town, constructing little canals and waterways from stream to stream. The town is therefore rich in little bridges; and I remember that as children we were immensely amused by some American visitors who declared that at night parts of the town reminded them of Venice. I now think that they were not so far wrong.

With its key position at the river junction, Wilton was an important place from earliest times. The borough is older than the kingdom of England, of which it proudly considers itself the parent. King Egbert's Proclamation of 838, which united the ancient kingdoms of Wessex and Kent, was dated from "Our Palace in Our Royal Borough of Wilton". At that time Wilton possessed its own mint, and our earliest existing Charter, granted by Henry I, merely confirms to the borough its ancient rights and privileges. So the Mayor of Wilton holds an ancient, honour-able and dignified position; and it was a pride and a happiness to me to be elected to it in the autumn of 1938.

I have a seat on all the council committees, and there is no part of the mayor's work that could be more interesting than this. These committees tackle the actual details of the work which is done on the council property, and their members are experts in the trades and crafts involved. I have now learnt how to line a well, to tile a roof, to dig a grave—all Shakespearean avocations, and yet not taught to the student of English literature. These committees strengthen my belief that a small council is a more useful body than a very large one. Its members are practical men, profoundly interested in every detail. To hear their discussions is like listening to artists talking of painting, or musicians analysing a symphony. The technical knowledge of experts is equally interesting on any subject.

But the Mayoralty can be considered from more picturesque angles than this. Our small borough has lately made some interesting connections with America. Mr. Robert Bingham,

53   Rural Mayor in Procession
(*From a Drawing by Rex Whistler*)

54 The Town Crier of Lyme
Regis

55 The Horn Dance at Abbots
Bromley

56   Salisbury from the Meadows

the American Ambassador, discovered that in 1229 an ancestor of his had been consecrated Bishop of Salisbury. The cathedral was actually in process of building, and the ceremony took place in Wilton church. This church by 1930 had fallen into ruins, and the ambassador restored a little chapel in the middle of the arcading, so that whole site became a centre of peace and of prayer. The ambassador died while the re-building was in progress, and the work was completed in his memory. The chapel was re-consecrated with truly mediæval ceremonial. The Bishop in cope and mitre, choir and clergy in surplices, the Mayors and Corporations of Wilton and Salisbury in their robes, the Brethren and Sisters of Bishop Bingham's Hospital on Harnham Bridge, twenty-five members of English, American and Irish branches of the Bingham family, marched in procession to the church, to the music of English and American hymns. It was truly an historic day.

We have also in the past few years made contact with our kindred towns in America. Alderman Moore of Wilton carried to Wilton in New Hampshire a bound volume containing many pictures of our town, and an illuminated address congratulating the American Wilton on the two hundredth anniversary of its foundation. And now Wilton in Connecticut and Wilton in Massachusetts, and other of our namesake towns, are offering to us unexpected and most heart-cheering sympathy and help during our time of war.

I should like to describe another picturesque and interesting ceremony which I have been very glad to revive while I have been mayor. Before the old church fell into ruins, close on a hundred years ago, loaves of bread used to be given away at its gate to the poor people at Wilton on every New Year's Day. Being Wilton's first lady mayor, I thought I might revive this custom and claim my privilege as the "loaf giver", for this I believe was the Saxon meaning of the word "lady". So each year I don my red robe and my chain of office and distribute bread from the church door. More than once the churchyard has been covered with snow during this ceremony, and this adds greatly to the beauty of the scene.

The population of Wilton is normally about 2,300, but since the war began this number has almost doubled. Schoolchildren, bombed-out families, civil servants, nurses and soldiers have crowded into the town, and are being cordially welcomed by its inhabitants. Each week I am amazed afresh by the hospitality shown by people possessing very small houses, to whom these unexpected guests mean every day an immense amount of real hard domestic work. This is a strenuous but very happy side of these years of war.

And now (1941) the town is preparing for enemy attack. More than a thousand years ago Wilton met and defeated the Danes who came to invade it and her inhabitants are now quite ready to meet the Germans. I pray that they may not be put to such a test; but should it come, I have complete confidence in my fellow-townsmen. May God help them to protect our town whatever may befall.

3   Country Women Then and Now

ABOUT FIVE YEARS AGO, THERE WAS PUBLISHED BY THE Oxford Press a small book giving great insight into the lives of country women in the middle of the eighteenth century. It is interesting to compare those days with our own. *Ann Cook and Friend* is an intimate and detailed record of housekeeping in more than one sphere of life. Ann and her friend were both upper servants in different country houses, and the book is a combination of a diary and a cookery book written by Ann herself. She describes the manner of living in the home of her master and mistress, and when she and her friend marry, we see the daily life of small professional people. Abigail, the "friend", married a prosperous architect's foreman who later became a successful farmer; while Ann's husband was an unfortunate and impecunious innkeeper. Looking back on those lives lived in the country two hundred years ago, one is at first inclined to believe that this must have been the Golden Age for housekeepers. It was not so. It was rather the Earthenware Age, and *we* might be said to live in the Tin Age. Ann Cook worked among *little pots, stewing pots, galley-pots, tubs, chests, delf, hash-pans, marble mortars, porringers, cullenders, brass-pans, earthen-pots* and *casks*.

Nineteenth-century kitchens had their dignity of burnished

57   Jam-making, Old Style

58   Jam-making, New Style

59   Turnip Tears

copper and brass, and they usually cooked in huge heavy iron saucepans; but we have taken to the more trivial metals. Frying-pans are mostly made of tin: we cook a good deal in enamel; but best of all we liked aluminium, until it flew over the moon to meet and beat the German aeroplane. Our store cupboards are filled with bottles and tins; and one of the boons for which we can thank the war is that at last we can persuade the salvage men to carry away our multitudes of tins.

During the Earthenware Age women were much more occupied with exclusively household tasks than they are to-day; and Ann Cook describes in great detail the kind of life they lived.

In her day, the housekeeper in a great house was a person of considerable importance and responsibility, as well as being a very hard worker. Ours, in fact, is the first generation which has definitely aimed at the reduction of labour. Before the machine age, good results were not expected without hard individual work; and if more work was to be done, the solution was to provide more workers.

The centre of gravity has changed since the eighteenth century. Domestic occupations then absorbed practically all the energies of country women. This is not the case to-day, and it is interesting to see what the change means for those most concerned.

Much of the glory has departed from country housekeeping. In Ann Cook's day, this was a noble art. Cooking did not begin in the kitchen, for Mrs. Cook well knew that the flavour of her poultry, when it reached the table, depended greatly upon the peaceful and pleasant lives lived previously by the birds. She was Queen of the Poultry Yard. When she went to market and bought what she called her "feathered flock", her purchases were at once introduced to her inflexible regime. Her birds were not carried home in baskets of such a size that they were compelled to travel lying on their sides, in which case "the stepping or trotting of the Horses makes them full of Bruises, and puts them into Fevers". So her poultry made the journey standing upright on their feet. At home, the separate broods were kept apart, "for as soon as mixt with Strangers, Battle-arrays ensued. . . . I have found by Reason of their Battles, their Heads have been so sore that they could not feed . . . the Conquerors got Bruises with their Wings flapping in the Coops with the battling". Mrs. Cook had no doubt that "intermixing with Strangers is bloody

11

Wars''. She believed that ''Poultry have the Sense of smelling, though they have no Noses'', so she surrounded them with pleasant scents. Once a week she drove her ''green Geese and Ducks'' to wash in the pond, which ''gave them great Pleasure'', as well as improving their ultimate flavour. Many hours every day were occupied by the feeding of her various flocks of chickens, turkeys, capons, ducks and green geese; and she ruled their lives with consummate majesty.

All this outdoor industry might seem to have been enough, but Mrs. Cook's indoor responsibilities were equally absorbing. She says that she ''resolved to rise early in the Morning, and never to exceed Six o'clock if I was in Health, nor to grudge rising two Hours sooner if I had an elegant Dinner to send up''. And her dinners were, indeed, more than ''elegant''. She often provided twenty or thirty dishes to a course, and most of these dishes were exceedingly elaborate. Ann Cook's ''Ragoo of Ling'' contained over twenty ingredients. She modelled the pastry sur-mounting her ''Hare Pye'' into the shape of a hare, ''setting the Hare on her Belly as she is in her natural Seat'': her ''Ham Pye'' was ornamented ''with various Shapes of Paste cut out, as wild Beasts and Flowers''. Being, as she said, ''a good Mechanic'', she made her sweets into ''Sham Turkeys . . . or any sort of wild or tame Fowl, and it may be a great Disappointment to some Gormandizers, and a very agreeable one to others''.

Besides this daily routine, there was the great business of preserving and conserving for later use. The family ''killed a Beef'' once a month; and then Ann stewed its ''Houghs and Necks'', as she did her Legs of Veal and her Chicken Bones, boiling them to ''a fine Glue, keeping it six Months, if necessary, with close sealing in little Pots, and if a Mess of Soop is wanted, I have it in a Minute''.

Mrs. Cook also made marmalades and fruit cheeses, ''Gellies'' and confectionery: she ''Mangoed'' her apples, pickled her beans, walnuts and mushrooms, and made a wonderful ''Cordial Hunter's Gingerbread'' which contained red port, brandy, cinnamon, race ginger, mace, cloves and nutmeg. She remarks that ''a small Piece of this is a Dram in the Morning''. No wonder.

Esquire Goodman and his lady were Abigail's employers. They were examples of the philanthropy of the eighteenth century, and everything which is now done by what are called the Social

Services was carried out in their village by these two people. Mrs. Goodman chose Abigail as her cook-housekeeper because she saw she would help her in the work among the poor. She said when getting rid of Abigail's predecessor, "I never liked this fliskey Girl that waited on me, for if she had brought me a Message of any poor Creature's Complaint, I see her Countenance turn sour". She gave Abigail her own old clothes, and allowed her to hire an under-cook at £6 a year, out of which she was to pay her own kitchen maid. Abigail writes: "No Servants upon Earth were more happy than we were of a worthy Master, a pious, generous and charitable Lady, whose Humanity was such that she fed the Hungry, cloathed the Naked, and was a great Doctress to them afflicted with Sickness". This excellent squire and his wife built a village school for forty children, for whom they provided clothes as well as education. They also clothed all the old people in the village.

Abigail was practically the district nurse of the neighbourhood. She writes: "As I was an excellent Horse-woman, and my Lady seldom wanted Patients, I arose two Hours sooner in the Morning than her Maid used to do, and had my little Pad saddled, so visited the Sick every Morning, always telling my Lady what Effects the Medicines had on them that had taken them; this was great Pleasure to her, for she said that my Judgement of the Sick exceeded hers".

When Mrs. Cook and her friend visited each other, their tea was "brought in in great Order". Then they dismissed the footman and agreed that as "Statesmen have private Interviews in Politicks, Merchants in Commerce, so let ours be upon the Art of Cookery".

Esquire Goodman had carried out a considerable amount of rebuilding on his estate, and while this was in progress, the architect's foreman, a "Youth of beautiful Person and Behaviour", lodged for three years in the steward's house. At the end of this time, Abigail says, "I received a Letter from him, the Contents of which set forth the Beauty of his Wisdom, and likewise the Purity of his Affection, which, in serious Words, declared that he was a Stranger to Love before, but has been captivated ever since he first beheld me".

Abigail insisted on another seven years' "Conversation in Letters" before she at last consented to marry him, and when the long courtship ended, it was found that the architect's foreman had a very comfortable home, with four feather beds, made from feathers carefully dressed by his wife whilst she was in service. Twenty-two yards of fine homespun linen, and twenty-two of coarse, made their sheets, and Abigail spun a "Web of Diaper" for towels, and one of "Hugaback" for tablecloths. The Goodmans established them in one of their farms, and their menage was ordered with great efficiency. The servants wore their best gowns in church on Sundays; and "as soon as Divine Service is over we all undress ourselves and put on our Homespun Gowns, so folds up our Clothes. For no Maid in the Family is allowed above one Gown washed in a Quarter of the Year".

On one side of Abigail's storeroom Mrs. Cook saw, on her first visit to the house, "five Partitions for bottled Wines, each containing ten Dozen of Bottles. She opened the Lids, took out a Bottle of each Wine, and called for five Glasses. 'Now', said she, 'taste the Wines, and give me your Opinion of them. There is Burgundy, French, Red Port, Frontiniack and sweet Mountain.' So tasting the Wines, which were all as clear as Rock-water, I said, 'If I had seen these Wines in a Gentleman's House or in any Tavern, they might have passed for Foreign, for they are strong, and must be of good age'."

From all this it can be seen that two hundred years ago a country woman took so much pride in her home that her work in it was completely absorbing. No one who was at all house-proud could rely on anyone but herself and her household to make her home as she wished it to be. This has been changed in the Tin Age. Housework has been immensely reduced by mechanical appliances. Jams are bought in shops. Meals come out of tins. As the advertisements say: "You press the button, we do the rest". Or " Take a book and read. Take your work and sew. Go and mind the baby. And the washer will do the washing".

So the country woman is now free for communal work, and she is turning to it with great ability. Those picturesque old village schools have unhappily disappeared, and we have in their place universal education, with all classes of women on their boards of managers. District nurses ride bicycles or drive their Baby Austins in the place of the ladies and their housekeepers on their little "Pads". The whole village helps with the nurse's fund.

But the chief sphere of women's work in villages is the Women's Institute. Cottage women are proving themselves to be efficient organisers, and this in a very short time too. It is not so long since I was present at a public dinner when the toast of "the Ladies" was proposed by the oldest gentleman in the room. He remarked on the great change in the position of women which he had seen in his lifetime.

"When I was a young man", he said, "the ladies never went out but once a year, and that was on Good Friday, when they used to go up to the old castle and play kiss-in-the-ring. And now," —he concluded dramatically, "they has votes."

It is indeed a contrast; and to exchange a good game of kiss-in-the-ring for the dreary solitude of a polling booth is a poor alternative; but the Women's Institutes have humanised the new regime. While they make country women more public-spirited, they simultaneously develop their social gifts. It is quite possible to ridicule the grimly "business" side of the Institutes—their Federations, their Groups, their Elections of Committee with secret ballot and tellers, their bundles of circulars containing National, County and Institute information. All this has to be solemnly tackled at the beginning of every meeting; but no one who has shared their work can fail to see that, within all this rather absurd formality, there has grown up a new and living spirit to inform village life. The Women's Institutes really are the village social unit. They welcome new comers, and make friends with them. They arrange the tea at the village flower show or cricket match. They collect money for the parish nurse. And then they revive all kinds of country crafts, basket-making, patchwork, embroidery, shoemaking, knitting, umbrella covering—these are their industries. They organise communal jam-making and fruit-bottling. They study gardening and home nursing. They train glee parties who compete in county musical festivals. They produce really good plays. They make cakes and cream cheeses which they sell at market stalls in the country towns. They are indeed re-creating the village life at a time when it had begun to flag sadly because of the fall in the farming population. Unless a means had been discovered of replacing the old self-sufficient cottage life of the days when housewives were entirely responsible for the health, comfort and entertainment of their families, village life must have died of inanition. The

Oxford Dictionary tells us that this word means "the action or process of emptying: the condition of being empty". Women's Institutes are filling the villages again with occupation and interests.

On most afternoons in the month a village street is a sleepy place. Hardly a soul can be seen. Fordingbridge in Hampshire goes to such an extreme in this direction that the inhabitants of the neighbouring villages aver that its people only get out of bed every other day. I can vouch for the bareness of its street on a good many afternoons in the year, but if I happened to drive through on the day when the Institute met, I should no doubt have a different impression. At about two o'clock, or else at six-thirty, in most villages, the doors now open all down the street. Out come women of all ages, shapes and sizes. Some push perambulators, some do not; some carry parcels of knitting or needlework; some bring baskets of cakes; one or two hug important looking bundles of minute books and typed circulars. The individuals merge into groups, the groups into a small crowd. The crowd swarms round the door of the village hut and is gradually absorbed into it. Inside, everyone has her traditional part to play. Some elderly members gravitate immediately towards corner seats into which they sink, never to utter (or seemingly to hear) a word from beginning to end of the meeting. Others rush to the kettles, or cut up the cakes. Some place copies of *Jerusalem* on the seats, or take charge of the lending library. The secretary has an important word for nearly every member. The president puzzles over documents from headquarters. The speaker or demonstrator nervously pushes open the door, to be welcomed by a member specially deputed for this part, who conducts her to a seat on the president's right. Bunches of flowers, knitted socks, cakes, pots of jam, home-made wines and collections of potatoes are displayed on the competition table. The sales table exhibits anything possessed by any member of which she would feign be rid at a cheap rate. The members cluster in groups, discussing all these things. The president calls them together in tones which vary from the vague and nervous to the feminist and efficient. *Jerusalem* is banged out on the piano, if one exists. If not a courageous member lifts up her voice to "start it"; with the result that the singers are swiftly heard to be either soaring and squeaking in the region of the "top C", or else are buzzing like aged bees in a honey-pot. It is noticeable that the members are generally far more comfortable in the bass than in the treble. The song ends with a long and sentimental rallentando. "Minutes" and "Business" are then dealt with; and now the speaker rises, making a brave effort to outshout the chorus of babies' voices which fills the room, giving to the gathering a thoroughly homely atmosphere. Tea is eaten. The "Social Half-hour" produces various odd games in which people run up and down between rows of chairs, or blow balloons at each other. Sometimes the members dress up in their grandmothers' clothes and parade about, wondering how it was possible that, two generations back, women could wear clothes which are too small even for the dolls of to-day. The skeleton of every meeting is of a rigid formality. It follows certain lines laid down by the Medes and Persians belonging to a mysterious organisation known as "the Federation"; but this skeleton remains completely invisible. Institutes are generally small enough to be entirely friendly; and the prescribed forms are no more hampering to this friendliness than the cups are felt to hamper the tea as it is poured into them at the close of the meeting.

And out of these little burbling informal coteries there arises a recognisable village personality. The Great House has too often passed from the family of its original owners. It may even have become an "Institution". The parson is sometimes shared with one or two adjoining parishes, so there may be no clergyman's wife to do the honours of the place, and to care for the poor and the sick. Women's Institutes are developing a sense of responsibility, enabling them to undertake much of what used to be done by one person, and the arrival of "the evacuees" has hastened the growth of this quality. The end of the war will see the Institutes stronger than ever, because of the tasks to which they are rising to-day.

4 From Mumming to Pageantry

THE PASSAGE FROM MUMMING TO PAGEANTRY IS MORE than a change in taste. Mumming is indigenous: Pageantry, as we know it, is exotic. When I was a child, there was a good deal of native talent in the countryside: it sprang spontaneously from the soil, and was not cultivated by connoisseurs. In fact, it was rather despised by the "educated classes". There were the Christmas Mummers, who always performed in the kitchen. There were true Folk Songs, handed down by ear in the villages, and sung in public houses. And in some places there were traditional dances.

All these things had been originally created by the village people themselves. By "professional" standards they were not very good. They were like the wild primitive plants from which all our cultivated varieties have been developed; and like other wild plants they had characters of their own. A strong growth. A powerful stink. Fewer flowers, and those with less vivid colours than their "garden" descendants. A difficulty about transplanting and a tendency to fade quickly when gathered and brought into the house.

In recent years, some of those local plays and dances have been revived by archæologically-minded fanatics of physical training. Some modern Morris-dancers are extraordinarily good, but they are trained by experts, and are not spontaneous. Originally, these sports were practised by the ne'er-do-wells of the village: now they are produced by welfare workers. They appear at county festivals. They are judged by professionals. They win challenge cups. The wild flowers have been transplanted into the gardens, to be improved out of knowledge. Yes, they have been improved. They are now danced accurately; yet there must always be something rather absurd in a team of district visitors conscientiously stamping through a Morris Dance, while the rude forefathers of the hamlet sit on a wall smoking and smiling as they watch.

Mummers are found in every county in England, and their play is obviously always a variant on one very archaic pattern. It must be older than Christianity. It grew out of some primitive Nature cults, and the clumsy games of Single-stick, of which it largely consists, were once a dramatisation of the myth of the Sun's

60, 61   Harvest Homes

62, 63　The Village Green

death in winter, and his rising again with the Spring Solstice. It is therefore akin to the stories of Demeter and Proserpine; though beside them, it moves in the farcical world of pantomime. On to this original stem was grafted a Crusader's Play, and the characters we see to-day are nearly all of that date—St. George, the Turkish Knight, and so on. All English history, as seen through the eyes of country yokels, has left its mark on the subsequent versions of the Mummers' Play. Robin Hood appears sometimes, and Wat the Tyler. There seems at first to be a purely arbitrary choice in the names of the battles which crop up in the play, but they are those battles in which men from a particular village took part, for each village had its own version. Indeed, if only one could follow all the allusions, much would be learnt of local history. The battles of the last war are often mentioned, and all the Mummers whom I have seen end their play with a dirge in honour of the Death of Nelson.

And now I will give the Mummers' Play as it was performed in Quidhampton before 1914. It then disappeared for a time, and I persuaded the old men who had last acted in it to let me take down the words as they spoke them. The play had never before been written down. It had been handed on for generations by word of mouth, and often had grown to be mere gibberish. When I asked the meaning of a phrase or a word, or, if it seemed quite meaningless, suggested a possible alternative, the answer always came:

"That's 'ow we 'ad it."

Each man knew only his own part, and no one knew the play as a whole; though the old man who used to carry the actors' coats could generally fit the parts in one with another.

THE QUIDHAMPTON MUMMERS' PLAY

CHARACTERS

BOLD SOLDIER. (*Wears an old military tunic.*)
FATHER CHRISTMAS. (*Traditional dress. Carries a broomstick with a bunch of holly and mistletoe on it.*)
KING GEORGE. (*Domed hat.*)
TURKISH KNIGHT. (*A little smoking cap with tassel.*)
CUT-THE-DASH. (*A sash worn across his chest.*)
THE DOCTOR. (*Black clothes; dress coat; cocked hat with feathers.*)
LITTLE JOHNNY JACK. (*Seven dolls hung across his back.*)

All the characters have their clothes sewn all over with different coloured cambric slashed into ribands.

12

Enter BOLD SOLDIER.

BOLD SOLDIER: Ah ha! The doors are open and we're now in.
We beg your favour for to win.
For whether we rise or whether we fall,
We'll do our best endeavour to please you all.
We're none of the ragged tribe, ladies and gentlemen.
We've come here to show you a little fight and pastime.
And if you don't believe the words I say,
Walk in Father Christmas, and clear the way.

Retires. Enter FATHER CHRISTMAS.

FATHER CHRISTMAS: In comes I, Father Christmas.
Christmas or Christmas not,
I hope old Father Christmas will never be forgot.
And now I pray you, ladies and gentlemen,
To give us room to render.
For we've come here to show you fight,
To pass away the winter.
A fight you've never seen before.
I'm the man that leads King George in the door.
Walk in, King George, act thy way, and show thy part,
And show the beloved company of thy wondrous art.

KING GEORGE *enters.*

KING GEORGE: In comes I, King George, lately come from town to town,
To show the greatness of my strength,
To show the feat of valour.
Dun cow and dun,
Likewise men's chastity.
To see two dragons fight,
And to kill an ugly creature
Is all my delight.
Ask for Bold Soldier. Oft of him I've been told.
I wish his ugly face I could now behold.

FATHER CHRISTMAS: Walk in, Bold Soldier, cut thy way, and act thy part,
And show the beloved company of thy wondrous art.

Enter BOLD SOLDIER.

BOLD SOLDIER: In comes I, Bold Soldier, Bold Slasher is my name.
'Tis I that fought the fiery dragon
And brought him to his slaughter,
And by that means I won the King of Egypt's daughter.
My head is bound with iron, and my body bound with steel,
And with my arms up to my knuckle bones
I'll fight King George to win his throne.
Pull out thy purse and pay;
Pull out thy sword and slay.
Satisfaction will I have of thee before I go away.

KING GEORGE: No purse will I pull out,
 No money will I pay.
 Neither shall thee give me satisfaction
 Before thee'st go away.

> *They fight.* BOLD SOLDIER *drops wounded.*

FATHER CHRISTMAS: O King, O King, what hast thou done?
 See, one of my soldiers lies bleeding on the ground.

KING GEORGE: You gave me the first offer, Daddy, how could I refuse it?
 Have you got another of your soldiers for me to conquer or to kill?

FATHER CHRISTMAS: Yes; I've another of my soldiers for thee to conquer or to
 kill.
 Walk in, the Turkish Knight,
 Go thy way and act thy part,
 And show the beloved company of thy wondrous art.

> *Enter the* TURKISH KNIGHT.

TURKISH KNIGHT: I comes in, the Turkish Knight,
 Come from a foreign land to fight.
 I'll fight this English champion bold,
 If his blood runs hot, I'll quickly draw it cold.

KING GEORGE: O Turk! O Turk! thou talkest bold.
 Thou talkest as other Turks, as I've been told.
 Pull out thy purse and pay,
 Pull out thy sword and slay.
 Satisfaction will I have of thee before thee'st go away.

TURKISH KNIGHT: No purse will I pull out,
 No money will I pay.
 Neither shall I give thee satisfaction
 Before I go away.

> *They fight.* TURKISH KNIGHT *drops wounded.*

FATHER CHRISTMAS: O King, O King, what hast thou done?
 See, one of my soldiers lies bleeding on the ground.

KING GEORGE: You gave me the first offer, Daddy; how could I refuse it?
 Have you got another of your soldiers for me to conquer or to kill?

FATHER CHRISTMAS: Yes; I've another of my soldiers for thee to conquer or to
 kill.
 Walk in, Cut-the-Dash.
 Go thy way and act thy part,
 And show the beloved company of thy wondrous art.

> *Enter* CUT-THE-DASH.

CUT-THE-DASH: In comes I, Cut-the-Dash.
With my broad sword and my fine sash.
Although my King is not here to take his part,
I'll take it with all my heart.
Now I've almost end my ditty,
I hope on me you'll all have pity.
Now I've almost end my story,
I hope the battle will end in glory.

They fight. He goes on his knees, not altogether beaten.

CUT-THE-DASH: I'll have no more of thy high words, nor none of they diddly dumps.
For now that thee'st cut my legs off, I'll fight thee on my stumps!

They fight again. KING GEORGE *wins.*

The three lie on the floor. KING GEORGE *walks round them.*

KING GEORGE: Behold and see the wonders I have done!
I've cut down my enemies like the evening sun.
(*To* FATHER CHRISTMAS): Call for a doctor as quick as you please!
Perhaps one of his pills may give a little ease.

FATHER CHRISTMAS: Is there a doctor to be found
To cure my three sons which lie bleeding on the ground?

Enter DOCTOR.

THE DOCTOR: Yes, there is a doctor to be found
To cure thy three sons which lie bleeding on the ground.

FATHER CHRISTMAS: Are you he?

DOCTOR: I am that.

FATHER CHRISTMAS: What's thy fee, doctor?

DOCTOR: Ten pound is my fee.
But full fifty will I have of thee
Before I set thy three sons free.

FATHER CHRISTMAS: Tut, tut, Doctor; none of thee foreign off talk.

DOCTOR: Yes, Father Christmas; I am a foreign off man.
I've travelled India, South India, and Bendigo,
And now I've returned to England again.

FATHER CHRISTMAS: Well; give us a sample of thee work.

DOCTOR: I carry a little bottle by my side
Which is called the Opliss Popliss Drops,
Which I touch one to the heart and one to the head.

(*He does so*).

I heal thee of thy wounds once more,
So please get up I pray.

(They all get up and mingle together fighting again, their swords mingled in a bunch. Father Christmas, with his holly bough, forces himself in among them.)

FATHER CHRISTMAS: I'll have no more of that fighting here.

Enter JOHNNY JACK.

JOHNNY JACK: Here comes I, little Johnny Jack,
With my wife and family at my back.
Out of eleven, I have but seven,
And three of them are gone to Heaven.
One to the Workhouse he is gone,
And the rest will go when I get home.
Although I am but short, and small,
I think I am the best man among you all.
What say you, Daddy?

FATHER CHRISTMAS: Yes, yes, my son.

JOHNNY JACK: Christmas comes but once a year,
And when it comes it brings good cheer.
Roast beef, plum pudding and mince pie.
Who likes that better than Father Christmas and I?
Each one of them is a very good thing,
And a pot of your Christmas ale will make our voices ring.
Right wheel! Quick march!

(They march in a circle with tambourine and concertina.)

All sing:
Christmas is the time for merriment,
Time for merriment,
Time for merriment,
Christmas is the time for merriment,
Christmas is the time!

They stand in a circle and sing:
Britannia long expected news from the fleet,
Commanded by Lord Nelson the French to defeat.
But when the news came over, to England it was layed,
The French were defeated, but Lord Nelson he was slayed.

They sing other songs, ending with "God Save the King".

Before the wireless had taught country people to listen to jazz bands from London hotels, there was a good deal of home-made music in the country. I am not now speaking of the young ladies who carried their portfolios with them to dinner parties and entertained the company with ballads and pianoforte pieces. It was true that they often did so, but there was plenty of music in other walks of life. Small parties of working men in Wilton used to meet on Sunday evenings to sing Handel and Haydn together. This was before local musical festivals had been heard of, and the parties met for sheer love of music, not in order to practise for an outside event.

I have also a manuscript book of glees and catches used by a little glee party in the neighbouring village. It is written in a very rustic hand, and has been much handled, pawed and used. The spelling is natural, not acquired. This is an instance:

> Care thou canker of our joys, now the tyrant reign is over
> Fill the mystick bowl my boys, revel all without controul.
> Mirth and all thy train come in, cast of sorrow care and sighs
> Seize the villian plunge him in, see the miscrant traitor dies
> O'er our merry midnight bowl, God shews happy we shall be,
> Day was made for vulgar souls, night my boys for you and me.

> Giles Jolt as sleeping in his cart he lay,
> Some pilfering villians stole his team away.
> Giles wakes and cries, A ha! What the dickens what?
> Why here now, am I Giles or am I not?
> If I am Giles, I'm sure I feel the smart.
> If not, Odds buddikins, I've found a cart.

The following catch is said to have "gained a Prize Medal":

> To the old long life and treasure
> To the young all health and pleasure
> To the fair their face with eternal grace,
> And the foul to be loved at leisure.

This is a graver one with a touch of grim humour:

> Look neighbours, look, here lies poor Thomas Day
>   Dead and turned to clay.
> Does he sure? What, young Thomas?
>   No. No.
> Does he sure? What old Thomas?
>   Aye. Aye.
> Aye, Aye, Aye. Poor soul.

From these fragments one can judge the kind of wit and humour which appealed to country people before their minds had been standardised.

At Abbots Bromley, in Staffordshire, they still dance a Horn Dance, the origin of which had probably been forgotten before 1125, the year in which some people mistakenly think it was first danced. On their heads the dancers wear enormous reindeer horns, with harness of wood and iron. The horns are painted red and blue and white, and the latest coat of that paint is said to date from the sixteenth century. In 1686 a detailed description of the Horn Dance appeared in Plot's *Natural History of Staffordshire*, and in 1915 the dance was actually danced in khaki. In that year there were at home on leave four young men belonging to the family which is said to have led the dance for 300 years. Their father was then too old and weak to "lead the horns", so the sons "took them out", while the father carried the "little white horn". When the horns are not in use they still hang in the church, to be ceremoniously carried out whenever they are to be used. Miss Marcia Rice, in her *History of Abbots Bromley*, says of the dance:

"It is not now, and it never has been, a 'sport' or a 'kind of amusement'. . . . No one who has seen the dance can think of it as anything but serious, whether deriving from Christian or Pagan days. It is, and always has been, a 'rite'. It is impersonal. It does not provoke amusement. It creates a sense of wonder and respect."

The Horn Dance must have the same origin as other Mummers' Plays, but its character as a ballet has saved it from degenerating into farce. It remembers its high ancestry.

The village of Great Wishford in Wiltshire possesses a manuscript of 1603 in which is written "A true recital of the old, ancient and Laudable customs" of the place. Among these "customs" is this:

The "Lords, Freeholders, Tenants, and Inhabitants of the Manor of Great Wishford, or as many of them as would in ancient times, have used to go in a dance to the Cathedral Church of our Blessed Lady in the City of New Sarum on Whit-Tuesday, and there make their claim to their customs in the Forest of Grovely, in these words: *Grovely! Grovely! and all Grovely!*"

A year or two ago there were still living in Wishford grandchildren of Nanny Trubridge, the last of the Wishford maidens who danced before the High Altar at Salisbury Cathedral. That

custom disappeared at some time in the last century; but the
Wishford people still troop to Grovely Forest on Oak-Apple
Day. There they cut their green boughs, and then they carry
them in procession round the village, the men in foresters' dress,
and the women with faggots on their heads. This is a kind of
ceremonial mumming; and I class it with the others because it
is a genuine folk survival, kept alive by the village people among
whom it originated. The war, so far, has not interrupted it.

Pageants are quite another story. They make no claim to be
natural growths and they are frankly theatrical, for they must be
necessarily on a large scale, and demand a producer efficient
enough to handle crowds. Skilled wardrobe mistresses and a big
orchestra are also required. In recent years there have been a
good many pageants. They are among the things we country
people do. The rehearsals are perhaps the best part of all, and
in this, pageants resemble other private theatricals. They also
give considerable amusement to their audiences, although this
amusement gets much of its flavour from a certain tartness in the
point of view of some of the spectators.

A pageant has usually some historical dignity. It is built round
the story of a great house, an abbey, a group of villages, or some
famous historical personage. Its trump cards are local descendants
of the chief historical characters. If enough of these are collected,
the pageant is bound to be a success. In the past few years we
have had several in Wiltshire. Longford Castle staged one in the
Tudor period—the time when the present castle was founded.
Lacock enacted a whole day in the life of its village and abbey
during the sixteenth century. Wilton produced a George Herbert
pageant, to commemorate the 300th anniversary of the death of
the poet.

Pageants demand a large number of players, and every class of
performer appears. At Wilton, the present-day members of the
Herbert family impersonated their ancestors: Tim Tillbrook,
the huntsman of the Wilton Pack, hunted his hounds over the
hill; Mr. Elliott, the Wilton tailor, was called in, as his predecessor had been, to measure George Herbert for his parson's
suit; the Bemerton villagers of to-day represented their forefathers, who stopped their various daily avocations when they
heard Master George Herbert's praying bell; Wilton people
stocked the stalls at their historic fair; and the oldest brewing

family in the neighbourhood produced from its cellars casks and bottles of the correct date. But perhaps the greatest *coup* of all was the appearance of the Dean of St. Paul's in the part of Doctor Donne.

From this summary of one pageant it can be seen that its purpose (like that of all the others) is to recall to life and to dramatise something which once really existed or happened in the place. Pageants have therefore a definite historical aim, although to most of those taking part, whether as performers or spectators, two other of their characteristics are more predominant. They give pleasure, and they raise funds for local charities. Country people are fortunate in being able so frequently to combine these two.

5 Some Country Pursuits

COUNTRY PURSUITS CAN BE DIVIDED INTO TWO CLASSES— those which are accompanied by noises peculiar to themselves, and those which are carried out in silence. Hunting brings with it a complete orchestra as well as a vocal chorus. There is the "Yoick!" "Halloo!" "Tally-ho!" of the hunters, the merry tune of the horn and the music of the hounds giving tongue. Shooting is less noisy, though the beaters come up like an in-coming tide and the keepers occasionally fling out a "mark over". Then there is always the cannonade of the guns. Football is a pandemonium of bawling and yelling, mostly coming from the spectators, and cricket is silent but for the thrilling click of bat and ball, and sometimes a sharp "how's that?" towards the umpire, who is generally so taken aback, he can't think what to say. Then again roars from the gallery. Tennis has a very individual set of noises made up of the curious "olde wordes" which traditionally register its score. Whichever of these games is being played, the people in the next county are pretty well bound to know about it.

Among the more silent pursuits, fishing comes first—that exquisite, meditative, poetic sport interrupted only by the whizz of the wheel and the ripple of the stream. It is more like dreaming

13

than living. Golf is nearly as quiet, for the players seldom break into yells of triumph or even of despair. They pursue their ball with an unshatterable concentration over a landscape which is often of miraculous width and beauty. Then there is the pursuit of wild flowers by botanical fanatics, who go from one end of England to another in order to be on a particular day at the particular spot where a particular blossom is timed to appear. Putsuing blackberries is sometimes accompanied by a good deal of noise—laughter from those who enjoy the sport, and shrieks of anguish from those who are being pricked; but the chase for mushrooms is, at least in England, a silent one. Champion mushroomists go out at five in the morning, and this is not the hour for a great deal of noise or hilarity. Secretively they pursue the magic moonlight discs which now furtively show themselves in the fields. In Ireland, however, I suspect the mushroom to be of a somewhat different habit. I have never gone mushrooming there, but I remember once staying in a country house in County Down, when the stillness of the night was suddenly interrupted by an outburst of the most terrifying and uncanny shrieks it has ever been my lot to hear. The whole party rushed into the hall in various forms of *déshabille* and with wild surmises as to the source of those banshee howls. The guests were anyhow rather an extraordinary mixture. There were the Irish hostess and her three children; a French and an Italian governess; a young Swiss girl; an Englishwoman; a Swedish boy; and servants of all types, ages and nationalities. The only person missing was the cook. It eventually turned out that the screams which had awoken us came from an unfortunate boy who had walked in his sleep, fallen out of his bedroom window and broken his arm. That is, however, not the point of this story, which is, that when next morning the cook was asked whether she had not heard the noise that had awoken everybody else, she answered:

"I heard it. I thought it was the kitchen-maid picking mushrooms."

Other county sports, which fall between the noisy and the silent, are swimming and skating, often practised on the same pools, the one in summer the other in winter. Bathers generally shout a good deal, though their shrieks are not inherent in the art of swimming. Their purpose is to tempt shivering and nervous onlookers to make a first plunge, and to declare that

64, 65   The Hunting Tradition

67 - The Gamekeeper To-day

66   The Old-time Poacher

the water "is quite deliciously warm", despite the green faces
and the chattering teeth of those who so loudly proclaim this
obvious lie.

The noises accompanying skating are generally not made by
the skaters, but by long lines of boys who completely spoil the
ice by sliding across it; though there is sometimes an outburst
of hearty laughter when an ominous crack is heard and somebody
falls in, to clamber dripping out.

Besides their classification according to their sound or sound-
lessness, country sports have different degrees of dignity, arising
in the first place from the way in which they appeal to one generation or the other.

Hunting and shooting come first in this social hierarchy, and
they are the recognised prerogatives of landlords and parents.
The master of the house allows that they are serious occupations.
County business is not fixed for hunting days. A three-lined whip
is as impossible to ignore as is a shooting party. Guests for these
sports are selected by the master of the house. They are not
"young" parties like those which meet for dances. Parties for
point-to-point meetings have the same dignity. Father and
mother have the first call on the spare rooms, a right which at
other times is not so unquestionably their own as it used to be
when I was a girl. Picnic luncheons for shooting parties and
point-to-point meetings are the only ones served by butlers. In
fact they are not really picnics at all, but functions. It is true
that the younger members of the family are allowed to share in
these officially sponsored amusements, but they appear as cadets,
not as hosts and hostesses.

Fishing is also a prerogative of fathers, though it has never
taken to itself the airs of the other two. It has a clerical, almost
religious, unobtrusiveness about it. Only on one or two days
in the year do the devotees of the gentle art make common cause
with the rowdy poaching element which always hovers, unrecognised and ignored, on the borders of the world of sport.
Those are the days when the river is being dragged for pike.
Then everyone joins in—schoolboys and schoolgirls, water
keepers and labourers, master and man, mothers and aunts.
Everybody who possesses one, dons a stout pair of waders, and
the others borrow or steal someone else's. Nets are stretched
across the stream; and at the appointed time these are hauled

on to the bank in a way which might remind one of the twelve Apostles, if one's mind were not diverted by the sight of eighteen pounders hurtling through the air as they are pulled out of the nets. The brave people catch these long-toothed monsters; the cowards flee. And there is fish for tea in all the cottages that afternoon.

The golf-ball is another quarry pursued by parents; for, as is well known, golf is the game for the old gentleman, be he squire, vicar or haberdasher. Golf clubs are comparative innovations in the English countryside, to which they were introduced from Scotland only about thirty or forty years ago. In this country good courses are still rare, although the game has become a regular country pursuit.

The next group of sports is admittedly the group of the younger generation. Cricket and football, tennis, swimming and skating—these are the young people's games. No father plays football, and indeed in the country this game is only the inter-village cockpit of the under twenty-fives. But nowadays, when people who play games at all play them in deadly earnest, the young cricketers and tennis players have all been coached by professionals; so if any fathers join in, they make it clear that they are merely left-overs from some ancient battlefield upon which they won triumphs unguessed-at by the sportsmen of to-day. Swimming is now the most fashionable summer sport for the young of both sexes. All self-respecting country houses possess swimming-pools; and in most villages there are also bathing-places where children practise the art which they nearly all learn at school. In winter there is skating on these same swimming-pools; but the good skaters have left for winter sports in the Alps, and those who remain in England are mere amateurs.

As the year goes round it brings its seasonal pleasures to the nursery too. In the spring little children pick flowers, and all through life this is indeed a perfect joy. Snowdrops and violets, primroses, cowslips and bluebells succeed each other as the goals of radiant sunlit walks or drives; and later on, there are the mushroom and the blackberry harvests which still are left for the children to gather. When I was a child, we used to go with the other children to glean in the cornfields; and we ground our corn into flour in an old coffee mill for which we prayed for months. Then, by a miracle, it appeared in the nursery; curiously enough this was at the same time the cook acquired a new one in the kitchen. Nowadays, the mechanical reapers leave nothing behind for the gleaner, in spite of the injunctions laid down in the Book of Leviticus. But I suspect that machines are completely illiterate, so doubtless they have never even read that "the corners of thy field and the gleanings of thy harvest" must be "left for the poor and the stranger".

The pastimes I have mentioned might, to the casual visitor, seem to be a complete life's occupation for most country people, but so far I have not recorded the chief one of all. It is a pursuit equally absorbing to all ages, classes, sexes, trades and professions. I speak of gardening. This is indeed "the purest of human pleasures" as Lord Bacon said long ago; and the reason why it is so completely satisfying is suggested in the opening phrase of his essay: "God Almighty first planted a Garden".

There lies the secret. Gardening is Creation. It is taking part in the activity of the Creator of the world, and this means perfection. "Be ye perfect," said Jesus, "as your Father in Heaven is perfect." So only creative work can fully satisfy the spirit of man.

It is hard to say whether is best—to succeed to a great and famous garden, already a completed thing; or to plan and make the garden of one's dreams. I have no doubt which I should prefer, for the first kind of garden contains not only the actual beauty which strikes the eye, but the added beauty of association and history to fill the mind. I would rather inherit Wilton than lay it out anew; and I would infinitely prefer to be the gardener of Hampton Court than the maker of the gardens of Delhi.

The people who own the great and famous gardens are always busy in them. A garden is a living thing, and it is in its nature to keep on growing. The heir to a beautiful garden becomes the youngest apprentice in a great staff. He has around him all those workmen who knew the garden centuries before his day: the Head Gardener is the Spirit of the Place, who has made it what it is, and will inspire him to fit his most adventurous works into the long and lovely tradition.

Still, for those to whom Heaven does not give the wonderful birthday present of waking up in a ready-made Eden, there are the almost equal joys of making a garden for oneself. In the country, someone is always doing this. Every time a new house is built in a village, a bit of field or woodland is reclaimed, to be laid out by ardent gardeners who go through all the thrilling processes of studying garden pictures, drawing plans, carrying cords and tape-measures from point to point, digging, Dutch hoeing, raking, rolling, weeding and watering. The man who makes his own garden from the beginning can certainly take a more personal pride in it than the man who inherits one, and it is an open question which gets the most pleasure.

Then there are the tiny gardens, the real cottage gardens where certain flowers always seem to enjoy living far more than they do in the garden of the great house. The Madonna lily is one of these. But hollyhocks and phloxes also love the narrow borders which lead from a cottage gate; and that most capricious plant the mignonette, blooms in them late into the autumn. Some kinds of chrysanthemums can only be called cottage garden flowers. You never see them anywhere else. Their colours are oftenest yellow and brown, though they are sometimes of a delicious washed-out mauvish-pink, like the old-fashioned cotton dresses of village children.

Lastly come the allotment gardens, which in war time are becoming the most important of all. These grow the most enormous turnips, carrots and vegetable-marrows, the last of which sometimes miraculously produce on their sides a picture in relief of the village church. The climax of the allotment year is the Annual Flower Show—a tremendous event in any self-respecting village.

So in every walk of life in the country, gardening is the chief and most general of occupations. Long may it continue so to be.

Social life among the real country people is chiefly limited to luncheons and tea-parties, as nearly everybody hates going out at night, except for something very important. Country functions of this kind are not wildly hilarious, and perhaps the most original one to which I was ever bidden was a luncheon party given by a cow. Cherry was not only a champion milker, but had perhaps had her head slightly turned by giving a broadcast, when she was very chary about letting her voice be heard, although the whole world could hear the streams of milk which flowed into the pail when she was milked at the microphone. This is the invitation she sent me to her party:

68, 69   Walled Gardens

70   Village Cricket

CHERRY

requests the pleasure of your company at

RED HOUSE FARM, AMESBURY

at her final milking

on completion of the 365 days world's record

at 12 noon on April 7th, 1939

LUNCHEON AT 12.30

R.S.V.P.

The gayest of cities could never rival that.

THE FIFTH MOOD

CONDITIONAL

71   The Village Pond

72   Spring on the Farm

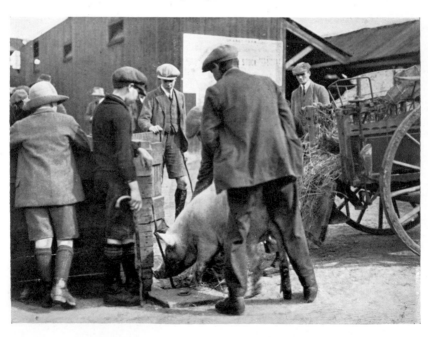

73   Farewell to the Pig

Conditional

WHILE I HAVE BEEN WRITING THIS BOOK, IT HAS GROWN ever clearer that the CONDITIONAL is the only Mood in which it is possible to contemplate even the immediate future. Life, as we have hitherto known it, has been sharply interrupted. The occupations, the pursuits, the pleasures, and the sports of which I have written in the preceding chapters, are nearly all in abeyance. Will country life ever be the same again? And how far do we wish it to be so?

At present one is overwhelmed by a nostalgic craving for the beloved old things; and then one has to remember that even before the war they were not exactly as they used to be. Legislation has long interfered, to a certain extent, with our happy-go-lucky ways. We rebelled against every fresh change; but now we believe it is patriotic to submit to conditions prescribed from outside. Being independent Englishmen, we retain at least the freedom to grumble.

"It's the war, so we must put up with it", we mutter, as we feverishly "fix the black-out" which obstinately refuses to remain fixed.

"It's every bit as bad as Hitler", we declare rather more loudly, as we learn that the very fruit from our own gooseberry bushes is to be turned into jam, not by ourselves, but by the Women's Institute. And they don't possess our grandmothers' unfailing recipe.

Again, "how can anyone expect ten self-respecting Buff Orpingtons to produce any eggs at all when they are fed on nothing but the scraps from a rationed household?"

Well, we are ready to obey orders to "win the war", but we do want to live our own lives afterwards, and the word "planning" begins to send cold shivers down our spines. It is true that nineteenth century *laisser-faire* doctrines produced economic, social and architectural confusion; but the twentieth century legislation has been by townsmen for townsmen, leaving

107

the poor countryman to fit himself in where he can. Perhaps after the war we shall find our one chance to arrest the landslide, but we must insist on taking our share in creating our own conditions.

By far the greater part of the soil of England is still agricultural, and if the greater part of its population has become urban, we are not therefore obliged to force the broad country acres through the slim needle's eye which fits the thread of city streets. Only country people know how much (or rather how little) legislation is needed to revive and preserve the attraction which village life has always held for the village freeman.

Consider the pigsty. Its acreage is small. Its importance is great. In my childhood every labourer possessed one, and on a Sunday morning the most familiar sight in a village street was the back of a man in shirtsleeves with probably three or four small boys beside him. They were leaning over the wall of a pigsty, poking the pigs with their sticks. These pigs were of immense interest to the family, and were a great topic of conversation between neighbours. They also consumed the kitchen waste, which is often a real problem in small villages. They converted this waste into bacon for the family, and nowadays they might have gone far towards making country places self-supporting. Pigsties might have been a main bulwark against the U-boat.

What, then, has happened to the pigsty? It was swept away by the new broom of by-laws created for towns, forbidding the keeping of pigs within sixty feet or so of a dwelling-house.

The pigsty is a symbol. It doubtless appears very small to an eye accustomed to those grand government offices in Whitehall, but it was a big thing to its owner. When it went, life became duller, as it moved another step away from Nature. The farm labourer lost his daily and most absorbing occupation, and he was offered in exchange a possible weekly cinema in a town several miles off, which he could only visit on those evenings when the motor-bus passed near his house. An occasional outing, however entertaining, can never make up for the emptiness of that pigsty, which was a perpetual occupation.

And no one with a first-hand knowledge of the two could possibly prefer a screen decked with film-stars to a sty full of little pigs.

To begin with, like other stars, they are completely remote. You cannot poke them with a stick, or feed them with the crumbs which fall from your table. Then, unlike the pigs, they give you absolutely no nourishment at all, and they don't address a word to you, or even give you an occasional grunt. So remote are they, that they are not actually there at all, and you are only looking at composite portraits made by skilled photographers. When these portraits speak, they converse one with another in a Hollywood accent which cannot be understood by the natives of English hamlets. Consequently the countryman in a cinema stares solemnly at scenes which have no power to draw out his mind: on the contrary they close it. He has no idea what it is all about; but there he sits, because he has nowhere else to go till the bus starts for home. As the mystic, absorbed in the presence of God, is lost to the events of the world outside, so, for the uneducated film fan, it is not necessary to know what the film is about. He is content to be rapt in the atmosphere of the god he has come to worship. And what a god!

This is no exaggeration. I once saw a Spy play with a party of young people; and, like my fellow yokels, I was baffled by the jargon of the American underworld in which it was played. From first to last I was completely at a loss.

As we came out, I heard my companions declare that they had never seen a better film, and with some embarrassment I confessed that I had not grasped which was the honest man and which was the spy. No one knew. They were all as much in the dark as I was, but this had not disturbed them. They had had a blissful evening, without vexing their minds to learn what they were looking at.

Present-day education of country children has not aimed at creating grown-up people who will make a good thing of country life: it is instead producing a generation of hungry and disinherited hangers-on to the edge of the nearest town.

Grace Stuart says, in her *Achievement of Personality*, that neurotics are those who have lost "the power to share an ordinary communal life", and they will never be at peace until they share it once more, "for that is the true end of the will". Rural education to-day may well create neurotics. From the age of eleven, children are taken from their villages to share in a more populous life outside. Their centre of gravity is disturbed.

Instead of living their own village communal life they become outsiders, trying to join in another one, to which they do not belong, where they feel they are not wanted, and where they are never quite at home.

"This feeling of inferiority", says Miss Stuart, "becomes crystallised as a great hunger for pleasure. . . . People with satisfying lives do not rush desperately and continually to the pictures. Nor do they keep themselves glued to their chairs at home by some superhuman effort of will. They quite simply do not need to go, and so they do not want to go."

Village life has been growing unsatisfying, and this at a time when, more than ever before, the nation has tried to assure to the young of all classes the birthright which is their due. The cost of national education has increased to an unbelievable extent; but we cannot be getting full value for that money if this education produces an unsatisfied generation.

We missed our opportunity in this country a few years ago when we were considering raising the school attendance age to fifteen years. We did not profit by the experience of other people and so made one rule for town and country. In several of the American states, town children after fourteen only go to school on 120 days in the year, and country children on 80 days; but it is obligatory that they have a regular occupation on other days. It is recognised that from this time onwards they are embarking on the career which will interest and occupy them throughout their lives. Alongside of this occupation it is compulsory that they should attend a continuation school for 400 hours in the year. In California this goes on until the young person is eighteen years of age.

In Switzerland the country children have a very happy time. From the age of twelve and upwards they only go to school in winter, and spend the summer on their parents' mountain farms, enjoying the life, benefiting by the open air, and practising the farm crafts which will ultimately give them their livelihood.

In parts of Denmark every child attends school for six days a week between November and May, while in the summer the elder children have only to attend once a week and the younger ones on two or four days. All the compulsory hours are worked off in the winter, and the summer lessons are extra ones. It has been found that this system is not only very popular with the

75 The Carter's Boy

74 The Ploughman's Boy

77   Into the Byre

76   The Puppy Fancier

pupils, but it produces scholars who can beat all town children in their final exams.

It will be seen that these systems must give considerable freedom to local education committees, and that is what we want here. Our county authorities should be allowed to devise schemes which adapt themselves to country life in the same way as do the educational systems in the countries I have described. Boys in our senior schools learn carpentering, but this is a very different thing from working with the village carpenter. It is merely playing. And no boy can learn in the school anything of the engineering crafts which form so large a part of modern farm life. Nor can he learn the actual work on a farm. There seems to be an idea afloat that to share in the work of grown-up persons means too hard a life for children: we have not forgotten the child-slaves of the early industrial age. But the open-air country work which I am advocating could be carried out under educational supervision; and no one who has seen the carter's little boys riding home with him after work can think for a moment that those children would have a better life if they spent their after-school hours staring in the shop-windows of a country town.

We have built our Central Schools and they must be used; but they should not wean the children away from the life of their own villages. A Central School may be located in a village, but it is not the village of the majority of the pupils. If we could evolve here something nearer the foreign system, our children could get the advantage of advanced book-learning in senior schools, but they could return to their own villages to work on the farm, or in the carpenter's shop or the blacksmith's forge. And every child prefers something real to do rather than to play at a trade in a class-lesson in school.

The first essential for reviving the English love for village life is to give back to the children their bygone property in it. Country life used to be the children's freehold. Modern education gives them in exchange a "lease and lend bill".

If something of this kind was made the aim of rural education we might help to restore to farm people the many skilled industries which they used to practise, and which made their lives infinitely more interesting than the life of a factory hand. We have not only lost our pigs, but we are losing the craft of dairying. No one may now make cheese or butter without complying with such conditions as would make the boldest farm worker quail. Yet, after the war, must it be for ever impossible to revive such a paradisal existence as that which Wordsworth once described?

"Towards the head of these Dales was found a perfect republic of Shepherds and Agriculturalists, among whom the plough of each man was confined to the maintenance of his own family, or to the occasional accommodation of his neighbour. Two or three cows furnished each family with milk and cheese. The chapel was the only edifice that presided over these dwellings, the supreme head of this pure commonwealth; the members of which existed in the midst of a powerful empire like an ideal society or an organised community, whose constitution had been imposed and regulated by the mountains which protected it."

It is to be hoped that the rural parts of England will not have to face the tremendous rebuilding problem with which the towns must grapple after the war. Yet some rebuilding there must be. Here and there farms and villages have already been devastated, and village churches have become ruins. But, apart from this, the process of regular rebuilding which always continues throughout the country has been checked. This happened in the last war, and to most people it was a great surprise to find what an immense amount of way had to be made up after four years during which the building trade was otherwise occupied. In 1939 we had not yet caught up with all our arrears and small local planning schemes were still being carried out. We shall have to do this again, and the way we do it will determine for future generations whether the England they grow up into is to be a beautiful country or not. There must be planning of some kind, and such planning should be on broad regional lines. It cannot be left to chance. Yet we don't want uniformity, which must ever be alien to the country spirit. I myself can conceive of only one unchanging rule. *Local materials must be used.* Then the country cottages of the future will belong to the landscape. They will grow as naturally into their surroundings as do the great prehistoric earthworks, which now seem part of the natural formation of the land in which they lie. It is only within the last fifty years that this rule has been broken. The thatched mud walls of Wiltshire, the stone-built Cotswold farms, the rough stone cottages

of northern England and the Scottish lowlands, which are sometimes whitewashed and sometimes painted in the yellows and
browns of the lichens which grow upon them—the timbered
and half-timbered houses of the Welsh border; the materials for
all of these were ready to the builders' hands, in days before
modern transport had revolutionised the roads. If these beautiful
materials were still utilised to build cottages, their interiors
might nevertheless conform to modern sanitary conditions. In
spite of its internal emphasis on good sanitation, it is not essential
for the exterior of a council house to look like a water-closet.

But we shall have more to do than merely build pretty country
cottages for farm workers. There must first, as I said, be regional
planning on a large scale. One lesson has been cruelly bombed
into us: our cities are too big. Such formless conglomerations of
houses as exist in the Midlands, or have even been casually
allowed to straggle round the beautiful city of London, with its
group of surrounding villages, are not only uncivilised, but
unsafe. They cannot be protected in modern warfare.

Heaven forbid, however, that we should re-plan our country
as if we expected only a repetition of what we are now going
through. My point is that these great cities are in themselves
like an east wind. They are neither good for man nor beast.
They should not be tolerated either in war or in peace. No one
seeing for the first time one of our large industrial towns would
believe that there was ever a day when the words "urban" and
"urbane" were almost interchangeable; and when a "city"
naturally indicated civilisation. There are districts in some of our
great towns where such ideas as civilisation or urbanity are simply
farcical.

The elephantine size of our cities has demonstrated that we
are after all a race of pygmies which has created, and cannot cope
with, a jungle of Frankenstein monsters compacted of bricks and
mortar. The first aim of our re-planning should be to make towns
in proportion to our size. Our industries will doubtless be quite
ready to scatter themselves more widely, now that modern fuel
inventions have made them independent of coalfields. So I hope
we shall have a considerable number of moderately sized industrial towns, planned as complete organisms, and not as
factories surrounded by cells; planned as Bath was planned, or
little Blandford in Dorset; or as Christopher Wren first planned

London after the Great Fire, when his intentions were frustrated by the vested interests of the City Companies, already, even then, for centuries in possession of the field.

Nothing can be more delightful than the small provincial town. These little industrial cities would be pleasant points of focus of the surrounding country. They would have their smokeless factories, and their streets and squares of artisans' houses; and they would also have their churches, schools, theatres, concert halls and playing fields. They should be frankly *towns,* not overgrown villages, and their inhabitants would be within easy reach of the "real country" outside.

But in addition to these country towns of the future, we shall, I believe, have to provide for many town evacuees who have discovered the charms of true village life. I know several town schoolboys who declare that, having spent these few years in the country, they will never return to the old life. They want to stick to the land, and if they do, they will bring fresh life to the farms. We have therefore a chance to arrest that townward trend of our population, which has been so disastrous for the health of the nation and so fatal to the farming industry. But we shall have to build good houses in the villages for these new comers; and we must give back their market to the village crafts and industries which are now being strangled by chain-stores. Village life must find again its old pride in itself.

Not long ago, I had a visit from an old-age pensioner, who could not write his name on the form he asked me to sign. He "made his cross". We had a good talk, and I found that he was a modern old fellow, who listened to the wireless every day, and said he didn't know what he should do without it. Then he went on to speak of his boyhood, when he had never seen the sea, never went to London, and only went to the nearest town with his mother two or three times in the year to buy clothes for the family. He described the fêtes in the landlord's park, the cricket matches, the amateur theatricals, the village concerts, the choir festivals and the flower shows. He finished by saying, "Don't you think we was more civilised then than what we be now?"

I saw what he meant. He remembered a community life, satisfying in itself, and without the inferiority complex which now prevents a village from doing things in its own way, because it hears so often that "they" do everything much better in town.

This snobbish attitude towards the town is no new thing, although my old-age pensioner was intelligent enough to be free from it. It existed in the days of La Fontaine, not to say in the days of Horace. *Le Rat de Ville* doubtless thought that his Turkey carpet set him several steps higher in the social scale than the *Rat des Champs* with his buttercups and daisies; but there came a common danger, which sent them both in search of country peace. Does not this recall memories of past months?

Here is the Fable:

THE TOWN MOUSE AND THE COUNTRY MOUSE

One fine evening the Town Mouse
Asked the Country Mouse to dine
In a fashionable house
Off remains of galantine.

On a handsome Turkey rug
The repast was neatly laid—
Never anything so snug
As the time our cronies had!

The regale was choice and rich
Everything correctly done;
But alas, there came a hitch
In the middle of the fun.

From the hall a sound was heard—
Was it an approaching foot?
Straight the host had disappeared:
His companion followed suit.

But away the footstep dies:
Back the timorous couple steal:
"All is well", the Cockney cries
"Come and finish up the meal."

"Nay, I've done", the Bumpkin said:
"Dine with me to-morrow night!
Not that with a royal spread
I can tempt your appetite;

"But at least I sup at ease,
Undisturbed by shocks like these.
Feasts, however aldermanic,
May be ruined by a panic."

Index

MADE AND PRINTED IN GREAT BRITAIN BY
WILLIAM CLOWES AND SONS, LIMITED, LONDON AND BECCLES.